BAD
TO THE
BONE

BAD
TO THE
BONE

THE PLAYBOY,
THE PROSTITUTE,
AND THE MURDER OF
BOBBY GREENLEASE

JOHN HEIDENRY

JOHN BLAKE

Published by John Blake Publishing Ltd,
3 Bramber Court, 2 Bramber Road,
London W14 9PB, England

www.johnblakepublishing.co.uk

First published in the USA as *Zero at the Bone* by St Martin's Press in 2009
This paperback edition published 2010

ISBN: 978 1 84454 871 2

British Library Cataloguing-in-Publication Data:

A catalogue record for this book is available from the British Library.

Design by www.envydesign.co.uk

Printed in Great Britain by CPI Bookmarque, Croydon CRO 4TD

1 3 5 7 9 10 8 6 4 2

Papers used by John Blake Publishing are natural, recyclable
products made from wood grown in sustainable forests.
The manufacturing processes conform to the environmental
regulations of the country of origin.

But never met this Fellow
Attended, or alone
Without a tighter breathing
And Zero at the Bone—

—Emily Dickinson,
A Narrow Fellow in the Grass

Also by John Heidenry

The Gashouse Gang:
How Dizzy Dean, Leo Durocher, Branch Rickey, Pepper Martin, and
Their Colorful, Come-from-Behind Ball Club Won the World Series—
and America's Heart—During the Great Depression

What Wild Ecstasy:
The Rise and Fall of the Sexual Revolution

Theirs Was the Kingdom:
Lila and DeWitt Wallace and the Story of the Reader's Digest

Contents

A Trusting Child

On the morning of Monday, September 28, 1953, Carl Austin Hall, a thirty-four-year-old ex-playboy just five months out of prison, and his forty-one-year-old mistress, Bonnie Brown Heady, a prostitute, woke up early. They had spent the night at Heady's home in St. Joseph, Missouri.

An old frontier town on a crook of the Missouri River, fifty miles north of Kansas City, St. Joseph, like Heady and Hall, had known better days. As the westernmost railway destination in the United States until after the Civil War, it had served as the prosperous gateway for settlers, miners, and others seeking their fortune on the frontier. It had also achieved a modest fame as the eastern starting point for the Pony Express, and considerable notoriety as the last hometown of the outlaw Jesse James. James had been living under the pseudonym of Mr. Howard when, on April 3, 1882, "the dirty little coward" Robert Ford shot him in the back as James, just before setting off to rob another bank, paused to straighten a picture hanging on a wall.

In the annals of infamy, a new chapter in criminal history was now about to be written unlike anything St. Joseph, or any other town in America, had ever seen. It starred sorry losers straight out of a bad pulp novel, and a child who lived a fairy-tale existence.

"It's very hot today," Heady remarked, as she got dressed.

A plump, big-breasted woman with red-tinted hair, a slightly bulbous nose, and oily skin, who stood five feet three inches tall, Heady was an ex-horsewoman and breeder of pedigree boxers and had fallen on hard times. Now, to make ends meet, she turned tricks in a glitzed-up bedroom in her modest suburban home. Trying to make herself look respectable, she put on her best dark brown gabardine skirt, a beige nylon blouse, a brown velvet hat, and white gloves.

Hall got into his blue sharkskin suit. Like Heady, he also came from a wealthy background, but had quickly squandered his inheritance on gambling, whisky, women, luxury automobiles, hand-tailored suits, and one disastrous investment after another. Reduced to robbing taxi drivers, he had been caught and spent more than a year in the Missouri State Penitentiary. During his stay in prison, Hall had completed his transformation into a hardened criminal, and whiled away the hours fantasizing about committing the perfect crime—the ultimate get-rich-quick scheme—that would enable him to retire to the wealthy community of La Jolla, California, and build a house with a circular bed that overlooked the Pacific Ocean. They would also travel widely in Europe, he assured Heady, the barfly hooker he had met just four months earlier, living off their investments and supplementing their income by playing the horses.

While finalizing the details of his cold-blooded, utterly conscienceless, and brilliantly simple master plan, Hall acted as Heady's pimp. Either he had not noticed, or ignored the fact, that she had fallen in love with him. She almost certainly did not realize that he cared almost nothing for her, and that her only value to him was to serve as an accomplice until he could dispose of her. Both were chronic alcoholics, each drinking at least one bottle of whisky a day. Hall was also addicted to amphetamines, and occasionally used morphine.

During all the time Hall spent rehearsing every last detail of his bold attempt to become wealthy again, he had overlooked only one small detail—his own unpredictable behaviour once he drank too much, and had money stuffed in his pockets. Back in his playboy days, that very combination had been his undoing.

By 7:30 Hall and Heady were on the road, taking with them her pet boxer, Doc. The dog was brought along so that casual observers might think it was the family pet. Heading down Highway 71 in her two-year-old Plymouth station wagon, they stopped at Lynn's, a tavern and package liquor store in North Kansas City, to muster their courage with a couple of shots. The tavern was the first on that particular highway between St. Joseph and Kansas City that sold liquor by the drink. Hall also insisted that Heady once again practise her lines, as they had the previous afternoon and evening. Before they left the tavern, he bought a packet of Clorets for Heady to chew so that her breath would not smell of alcohol.

By 8:50 they were parked outside the French Institute of Notre Dame de Sion, an exclusive Catholic elementary school in Hyde Park on the Missouri side of Kansas City. Hyde Park was a once fashionable neighbourhood that had slowly begun to decline after the end of World War II, as affluent families moved to the suburbs. Many of its large old Victorian, Queen Anne, and Prairie School homes had been converted into apartments and boarding houses. Yet the French Institute remained a sturdy and stylish presence, with a reputation for providing young boys and girls with both a first-rate education and sound religious formation that appealed to the well-to-do Catholic parents who enrolled their children there. Although subjects like history, science, and mathematics were taught in English, other subjects, including French, religion, and penmanship, were conducted in French, as was playtime.

As Hall and Heady watched, an elderly man named Robert

Greenlease drove up in his brand-new blue Cadillac, as he unfailingly did every school-day morning, and dropped off his six-year-old son, Bobby. Satisfied that they could now proceed with their plan, the pair drove to the city's downtown area, parked in the lot of Katz Drug Store at 40th and Main Streets, and waited. A little after 10:30, Heady walked to the nearby office of Toedman Cabs, got into a taxi, and asked to be taken to the school. When it pulled up at the French Institute at 10:55, she told the driver to wait, walked up the steps, and rang the bell. A French nun, Soeur Morand, who was the portress, or keeper of the door, answered. The school kept the front doors locked and was generally careful about visitors. But Heady, perhaps simply because she was a woman, aroused no suspicion, even though she fumbled her part several times despite her repeated rehearsals.

Appearing upset, she told Soeur Morand that her sister Virginia, little Bobby Greenlease's mother, had suffered a heart attack.

"How did it happen?" the nun, visibly distressed, asked.

Heady replied that the two of them had been shopping at Country Club Plaza, the city's most fashionable shopping centre, when she collapsed. Now Mrs. Greenlease was in the hospital and wanted to see her children, including Bobby, her youngest boy.

Thanks to extremely good luck and not to any careful planning on their part, Hall and Heady had chosen to snatch Bobby Greenlease from school on one of those rare days when every circumstance that might otherwise have thwarted their plan worked in their favour. Notre Mère Irene, the mother superior and a worldly wise American, was not in her office but away on an errand. She would easily have seen through Heady's impersonation of Virginia Greenlease's sister and summoned the police. The second in command, Mère Marthanna, was not only an American but also a Kansas City native. She, too, would have proved more than a match for the self-conscious, insecure Heady, but at that moment she was teaching a class. That left mild-mannered, sweetly innocent Soeur Morand temporarily in charge of greeting and vetting visitors. Although she spoke English quite well, Soeur Morand simply lacked the probing temperament that would have been second nature to someone in authority—to wonder why, for example, a woman taken to a hospital after suffering a heart attack would improbably ask to see her children.

Bobby's older sister, Virginia Sue, had only recently transferred from the French Institute of Notre Dame de Sion to another school. She also would instantly have known that Heady was not her or Bobby's aunt.

Soeur Morand suggested that Heady say a prayer while she went to fetch Bobby. As the nun led her visitor to the chapel, Heady blurted, "I'm not a Catholic. I don't know if God will answer my prayers." If Soeur Morand had been the least bit suspicious, the plot to kidnap Bobby would have unravelled right there and then, since the Greenleases—including, presumably, Virginia Greenlease's "sister"—were devout Catholics.

As Heady made her way to the chapel, a nun who had been cleaning the hallway happened by and thought the visitor seemed unfamiliar with the school. But as she spoke only French, she said nothing. Another nun, Soeur Alphonsina, also passed by, thought Heady did not at all resemble Mrs. Greenlease, and wondered if perhaps she was a sister-in-law.

"Are you Miss Greenlease?" she asked, in heavily accented English.

"I don't understand you," Heady, nonplussed, replied.

The nun continued on her way, and Heady once again avoided a potentially awkward moment that might have thwarted the kidnappers' plans.

Soeur Morand had gone up to the second floor to Bobby's first-grade Latin class. The nun conferred with the teacher in French, and then summoned Bobby, telling him that his aunt was downstairs, but without mentioning that his mother was ill. Bobby put down his books, but asked the teacher if he could take his Jerusalem medal with him; only two students had won one so far that year. Bobby left the classroom wearing it on a red ribbon pinned to his shirt, and he also took with him a mechanical Eversharp pencil imprinted with the name of one of his father's companies, Greenlease-O'Neill Oldsmobile. "We're going to see Mama," the nun reassured him.

By now Heady had come out of the chapel and met Soeur Morand and Bobby at the foot of the stairs.

"I'm not a Catholic," she again foolishly told the nun, "but I hope he heard my prayers."

"I'm sure he heard them," the nun answered.

Bobby, though he had never seen Heady before, walked out of the school holding her hand. "He was so trusting," she later remarked.

During the return trip to Katz Drug Store, Heady gently interrogated the boy, asking him, "Bobby, what are the names of your two dogs?" She also asked him for the name of his black parrot. Dutifully, Bobby answered her questions, even though the parrot was green, not black. He also told her that his family had two Cadillacs.

Heady explained to Bobby that they were not going to see his mother, after all, but his father. First, though, they were going to stop to get some ice cream. Hall was waiting for them in the station wagon when they arrived at the drugstore parking lot. Heady paid the eighty-five-cent fare with a dollar bill and told the driver to keep the change. Hall greeted the youngster with the words: "Hello, Bobby, how are you?"

"Fine," Bobby replied.

Heady and Bobby got into the front seat with Hall and they drove off, heading west on Westport Road to State Line Road, then south into Kansas to Highway 50 and west to Highway 69, skirting through Overland Park. Bobby, still trusting the two strangers simply because they were adults, never complained or suspected that anything was wrong.

At the intersection of Highway 69 and 95th Street, also known as Lenexa East Road, Hall turned in to 95th. They were now in Johnson

County, nearly five miles west of the Kansas-Missouri border, and about twelve miles from downtown Kansas City. Heading down a lane belonging to the Moody family's farm, Hall followed the ruts of a tractor until he came to an isolated spot concealed by crops and a windrow—hay gathered up on a rake to dry—and stopped. Hall thought Bobby seemed interested in the ride and was enjoying himself. Chatting happily, the boy observed some large green hedge balls and Heady offered to get him some. Hall quickly got out of the car to unlatch the tailgate and let Doc jump out. Heady, eager to be as far away as possible from the gruesome scene about to unfold, nervously trailed after the dog as it frolicked away.

Hall's first order of business was to smooth out a sheet of plastic—Bobby's shroud—that he had stored in the back of the car. He then went around to the passenger side and sat down next to the boy. His plan was to strangle his young hostage right away. But stupidly the murder weapon he had brought with him to accomplish that cruel task was a length of clothesline scarcely more than a foot long—not enough for him even to get a good grip on.

Bobby, perhaps growing suspicious that two people he did not know had brought him to such a lonely place, reacted violently when Hall tried to slip the rope around his neck. Kicking and screaming, he fought back furiously, but Hall managed to keep the boy within his grasp.

Finally, in exasperation, he threw Bobby to the floor of the car, held him down with both feet, and drew his .38 calibre revolver. Cursing and sweating profusely as Bobby continued to kick wildly, Hall struck the boy in the face with the butt of his gun. The blow knocked out three of Bobby's front teeth. Hurt and briefly stunned, he grew quiet—just long enough for Hall to take aim and fire. But the shot missed, ricocheting off the floor into the panel of the left door. He fired again. This time the bullet entered Bobby's head about one and a half inches behind his right ear, and exited two inches above the left ear, killing him instantly.

When the two shots rang out, Doc started to bark and leap about. While trying to restrain the dog, Heady lost her brown velvet hat—one she had bought years earlier at a hat shop in New York—and only much later realized that it was missing.

Hall dragged Bobby's lifeless body out of the car and laid it on the ground. After he wrapped the body in the plastic sheet, he and Heady lifted it into the back of the car and covered it with an old comforter used for the dog. Blood and brain tissue were splattered all over the front seat and floor, as well as on Hall's face, hands, and suit. Heady helped him remove the jacket, which he folded inside out and placed in the car. He rolled up the sleeves of his shirt, which was also covered with blood, and Heady used Kleenex to wipe his face and hands. She also picked up his glasses and the holster to his gun, which were lying on the ground, and put them in the glove compartment. Then they turned around and headed back to Kansas City.

"Why did you have to shoot him?" she demanded irritably. "I thought you were going to strangle him."

"I tried to," he replied, "but the goddamned rope was too short. Goddamn it, he was fighting and kicking. I had to shoot him."

At 11:30, Mère Marthanna finished teaching her class and was immediately told that Bobby Greenlease had been taken from school. She asked Soeur Morand for the name of the hospital where the boy's mother was being treated, and the poor nun replied that she did not know. She had not even thought to ask. Mère Marthanna went directly to the phone to call the Greenlease residence to find out the name of the hospital and to inquire about Mrs. Greenlease's status. Virginia Greenlease herself answered the phone.

"How are you feeling?" a surprised Mère Marthanna asked.

"Why, just fine," Mrs. Greenlease replied.

1.

Kansas City Noir

A granite obelisk stands in the cemetery of Trading Post, the oldest continuously occupied settlement in Kansas, about seventy-five miles south of Kansas City near the Missouri border. The historical marker commemorates the slaughter of innocent civilians in the so-called Marais des Cygnes Massacre, one of the bloodiest incidents in the Kansas-Missouri border struggles in the years preceding the outbreak of the Civil War. On the morning of May 19, 1858, Georgia native Charles Hamelton led a band of pro-slavery Missourians to Trading Post, captured eleven Free State settlers, and marched them to a nearby ravine. Hamelton fired the first shot, and then ordered his men to execute the rest. Five men were killed, and five others were wounded and left for dead, though they survived. The eleventh man, Austin Hall, escaped injury by feigning death.

Word of the massacre horrified the North. Abolitionist John Brown arrived at the site a few weeks later, and built a rudimentary log "fort," where he and several of his followers remained throughout that summer, lusting for a return engagement and revenge. John

Greenleaf Whittier, the abolitionist poet and Quaker, immortalized the dead in his poem "Le Marais du Cygne," published in the September 1858 issue of *The Atlantic Monthly*. He wrote:

> *A taint in the sweet air*
> *For wild bees to shun!*
> *A stain that shall never*
> *Bleach out in the sun!*

Austin Hall later became one of Trading Post's most prosperous citizens. His son John grew up to become an attorney and a community leader in nearby Pleasanton, a town named after Union general Alfred Pleasanton, whose population of 1,300 made it the biggest in Linn County. Known for its hunting and fishing, the county lies midway between Kansas wheat country and the Missouri corn belt. John Hall married a judge's daughter, Zella Cannon. They lived in a spacious, multistoreyed house on 311 West 10th Street. John Hall was regarded as an exceptional lawyer, but also as an uncompromising man of stern principles. He once successfully defended a client accused of murder, but his fee was the man's entire six-hundred-acre farm. The Halls' first child, a boy, sustained a brain injury during his birth and at age three was placed in a mental institution. He died two years later. The second son, born July 1, 1919, in Kansas City, Missouri, and baptized Carl Austin, grew up to be the wealthy couple's spoiled only child.

Carl's grades in elementary school were average, and he never attracted special attention. In 1932, just before Carl's thirteenth birthday, his father died suddenly of a brain tumour. That summer, Zella arranged for her increasingly unruly son to stay for a time with Pansy McDowall, a childless elderly widow who lived on a fifteen-hundred-acre ranch and had a reputation for helping raise children who had lost one or both parents. One night, McDowall found Carl sobbing in his bed and took him in her arms. He told her that he missed his father, and also his mother and maternal grandmother, whom he called "Tomama," for "two momma."

McDowall later characterized Zella Hall as "the most cold-blooded and hardest-hearted mother I have ever known." Carl, she remembered, though always courteous, was "quite a problem."

In subsequent years, Zella ignored and doted on Carl by turns, but mostly busied herself in the town's social life—women's clubs and civic activities. She was also active in her local Presbyterian church. One summer, in a bid to keep her son occupied, she persuaded the manager of the local telephone company to hire Carl as a telephone lineman at her own expense. The company had no need of extra help, but Zella wanted him off the streets from Monday through Saturday, and reimbursed the company's payroll department.

Most of his classmates went on to the local public high school. Carl wanted to go there as well, but Zella sent him to the Kemper Military School one hundred miles away in Boonville, Missouri. By now, the troubled teenager was frequently getting into mischief, going with friends to Fort Scott and other nearby towns to pick up girls and get drunk. Hall boasted frequently of his exploits with women and occasionally wound up in jail for disturbing the peace. But Zella had her own convenience to consider. Having a rebellious adolescent son to look after interfered with her social life.

Boonville, built on a limestone crest overlooking the Missouri River, marked the point where the Ozark upland trailed into the western plains. Named for Daniel Boone, who spent his last years and died in the state, the town prospered in the early nineteenth century when immigrants heading west disembarked on river ferries there, and then turned west in their prairie schooners for the overland journey. German immigrant Frederick T. Kemper had founded the Kemper Military School—initially known as the Boonville Boarding School—in 1844 with just five students. By the end of the academic year, enrolment had grown to fifty.

In 1899, the school officially changed its name to the Kemper

Military School, and began advertising itself as the "West Point of the West." Students, both male and female, even wore West Point–style grey uniforms. Humourist Will Rogers, its most prominent alumnus, attended the school in the 1890s. By the time Hall enrolled as a freshman in September 1933, the student body numbered about 450, with dress parade held every Sunday afternoon if weather permitted. Despite the severe financial hardships brought on by the Great Depression, the school still managed to build a new stadium and football field during this period.

Hall remained at Kemper for three years. One of his classmates, though they were not close friends, was Paul Robert Greenlease, the adopted son of a wealthy Cadillac dealer in Kansas City. At first Hall's academic record was good. Comments in his file, for his first year, included: "On honor roll one month. Member of rifle team. Member of company basketball team." In his second year: "Dependable, conscientious, promising cadet. Very likeable boy [but] slow developing. Good mind, willing to work, but temperamental. Honest and dependable. Fine youngster, dependable, capable and ambitious. A kid with [a] capacity for affection. Member of company basketball team."

In his third academic year, 1935–1936, Cadet Hall took a turn for the worse. File notes from instructors included: "None too straightforward. Has ability but must be observed constantly. A worthless streak at times . . . Tries to bluff; authority must be shown over him." He was also hospitalized during this period for an unspecified illness, and a note in his file observed that Hall "had attempted to have liquor brought into him."

It also so happened that, in 1935, the nation was in the grip of the sensational trial of Bruno Richard Hauptmann, who was ultimately convicted of kidnapping and killing the twenty-month-old son of Charles Lindbergh. Hauptmann was executed in April 1936. Like millions of other Americans, Hall almost certainly was familiar with the case—the most sensational crime ever committed in the United States. The nation's newspapers and the still relatively new medium of radio covered it around the clock. Just seventeen years later, Hall was to take his place in the annals of crime as the principal figure in a kidnapping case second only to the Lindbergh as the nation's most notorious.

Hall left the school in 1936 and returned to Pleasanton, where he attended a local high school in his senior year and was elected vice president of his class. In the fall of 1937 he enrolled at William Jewell College in Liberty, Missouri, a coeducational institution run by the Missouri Baptist General Association and named after the wealthy physician who had donated the land and initial endowment. Three months later, he dropped out. A family friend was later to recall that he got an underage girl in Fort Scott pregnant, and that criminal prosecution was avoided only after Zella Hall paid the family $2,000 to keep quiet. At his mother's insistence, the obviously troubled young man signed up with the U.S. Marine Corps, enlisting in January 1938 for a four-year tour of duty.

Hall's letters home were a chronicle of both a failing relationship between parent and child that was never to be repaired, and of his own free fall into increasingly reckless and irresponsible behaviour. Early on, writing from San Diego on March 11, 1938, he played the good son, telling his mother:

> I am positive that everything is going to be the way that they should be between a mother and her son. I now realize just how childish and demanding I have been, and I am truly sorry for the way I have acted. . . . I have definitely made up my mind, mother, that I want to study towards a law career. . . . All my love and kisses to you and Tomama.

By July 1941, life in the Marines had proved insupportable, and Hall wrote:

O, thank God! I am drawing nearer every day to getting out. I
am going to put every dime I can get on an apartment as soon as
I get up, so that I can get away from the barracks at night and
sleep in a good bed where there is a little piece [sic] and quiet.

Often broke, he telephoned Samuel Tucker, his mother's friend
at the Pleasanton telephone company, asking him to intercede with
Zella and urge her to wire him funds. Mrs. Hall, who was in
failing health, silently listened in on some of those calls, and
afterwards directed Tucker either to send her son the money, or
to ignore him.

Hall served four years in the Marines as a telephone equipment
lineman before being honourably discharged as a private first
class, earning an "excellent" rating from his commanding officer.
He then reenlisted, and served another four years. Given his
antipathy for barracks life and his eagerness to return to civilian
status, the only plausible explanation for his reenlistment was that
his mother—whose considerable estate he stood to inherit—insisted
on it.

Almost immediately, though, Hall found himself in trouble with
the authorities, usually for being drunk. In a letter postmarked
August 23, 1942, he did not hesitate to grovel:

I want to wish you a very *wonderful & happy* birthday. I would
have sent a telegram but was flat broke. Most of my
punishment was in form of a heavy fine. I am so plowed under
with financial obligations, I hardly know where to turn. . . . I
heard directly that I was going to be shipped to *New River, N.C.*
and be there about a week—enough to draw *gas masks*, etc.—then
aboard a *transport ship* and to one of the Islands to fight the
Japs. . . .

Mother, if you will I will appreciate no end if you could send
something. I know I shouldn't but you're my only turn to, and
also I'll see if you have forgotten me. Please send me a wire

either telling me you'll help me or not—because on the strength of that, I may be able to borrow enough money to tide me over till I get your air mail letter.

A letter postmarked September 14 and sent on the stationery of the Hotel Van Rensselaer in New York thanked his mother for ignoring his request:

I am glad you didn't send me the money I asked for—I would probably be in more trouble than I now am in if you had. I am so sorry I have caused you so much grief and trouble, dear, but I guess I just wasn't man enough to let liquor alone. If you disown me, I can't blame you. I am not fit to use the family name. God knows what punishment I'll get but I rate everything I get—only sorry I could not learn from previous lessons, but I guess I am a little crazy.

This time, instead of having to pay a fine for being drunk and AWOL, Hall was court-martialled and sentenced to serve time in the U.S. military stockade in Quantico, Virginia. During his incarceration, Zella Hall redrew her will, disinheriting Carl and naming his grandmother Tomama as her principal beneficiary. Writing from prison, in an undated letter, Hall sarcastically told his mother:

I never thought that anyone or anything could change your mind to such an extent that you would disown your only son. I know that you went to the city and had your will changed where I wouldn't get anything—or if I do get any little pittance I will be too old to put it to an education or any business. Life is so short anyway and everything is so uncertain nowdays that I can hardly understand.

Yes, I know I have been a criminal and everything horrible. My, but I must be terrible, much worse than I thought, to warrant this. However there are two sides to every question, and of course I don't guess you can understand what this outfit can do to one. . . . Wonder what father would say. . . .

Goodbye. I will always love you though you have disowned me. I know that you were influenced. If you don't write I'll understand.

Never forget—no matter what you can do, I'll someday be a credit to my father. He only left one son, but it's not too late for said son to do something, even though his mother didn't think so.

After serving his sentence at Quantico, Hall was sent to the Pacific with the 7th Regiment of the 1st Marine Division, and saw almost continuous action for twenty months in New Britain and the Solomon Islands. During this period, he earned several decorations, including two Bronze Stars. In September 1944, he took part in the assault landings against enemy positions on Peleliu Island, and later on Okinawa. Zella Hall died while her son was fighting in Okinawa, bequeathing $200,000 in stocks, bonds, and real estate (roughly the equivalent of slightly more than $3 million in today's money) to her mother. The estate included the Halls' family home and 1170 acres of prime Missouri and Kansas farmland.

Although Hall was again promoted, this time to corporal, in April 1945, he was also disciplined six times, mostly for drinking binges, and he was AWOL on four occasions. In January 1946, he was discharged "under honourable conditions," which was less than an honourable discharge. He had made sergeant but was demoted back to corporal for being absent without leave. By now the stockily built Hall, who stood five feet ten inches, had become a chain-smoking alcoholic who drank a fifth of whisky every day. He also became addicted to Benzedrine, an amphetamine that some pharmacists sold under the counter. Known colloquially as "bennies," amphetamines produced a feeling of exhilaration and temporarily banished fatigue, although aftereffects included heightened fatigue, insomnia, and possibly even suicidal tendencies. Dieters and long-haul truckers used amphetamines to curb their appetite or stay awake for long hours. When asked how he obtained bennies, Hall once explained that his technique was to hand a druggist a $20 bill and say, "This is my prescription."

Now a civilian and unencumbered by a disapproving mother, Hall was also, suddenly, a wealthy man. His grandmother died, leaving him the bulk of the estate Zella Hall never wanted him to have. Returning to Pleasanton, he quickly converted his real estate and stock holdings into cash, telling Marshall K. Hoag, a lawyer who handled his affairs, "Sentiment doesn't mean a damn thing to me." He also complained, "People got their noses up at me. They're jealous because I got money. I'll show 'em how money and brains can really get goin'." He was twenty-six at the time.

He also paid a visit to Samuel Tucker. Hall's father had owned $10,000 in preferred stock in the telephone company. Hall informed the older man that he wanted to sell it. Two days later, he returned to the office, picked up the check without looking at the amount, and simply walked out.

Hall's first stop was downtown Kansas City, which compared to Pleasanton was the big time. He took a suite at the Hotel Phillips, a posh Art Deco masterpiece. Tropics, its third-floor lounge, was particularly popular with salesmen and soldiers. Periodically, guests were treated to the sound of piped-in thunder and fluttering lights, signifying a brewing tropical storm. When the lights went out, a mechanical hula girl emerged from behind the bar, swaying in a grass skirt, while a simulated thunderstorm poured down behind her. Hall was a regular.

Like other cities around the country, Kansas City was also benefiting from a post-war economic boom. With a population of about 350,000, it now boasted the world's leading hay market and seed distribution centre, and the country's second biggest livestock market. A major railway hub, second only to Chicago, Kansas City was also known for its jazz, speakeasies, and criminal elements.

The city's political boss, and the man who hand-picked Harry S. Truman, then a local judge, to run for the U.S. Senate in 1934, was Thomas J. Pendergast, chairman of the Jackson County Democratic Club. On the day Truman was elected, four people were killed at the polls.

A modern-day Robin Hood, Pendergast distributed Thanksgiving and Christmas dinners to the poor, and helped the needy by paying their medical bills and providing them with jobs. Those voters were expected to express their gratitude with a 100 percent turnout on election days. Pendergast's efficient bribery system also ensured that Prohibition was virtually ignored in Kansas City. Gambling was widespread. Pendergast's corrupt, often violent, regime lasted from roughly the beginning of the century to his conviction for tax evasion in 1939.

One of Kansas City's darkest chapters occurred on June 17, 1933. That morning, in what later became known as the Union Station Massacre, Charles "Pretty Boy" Floyd and two associates tried to free Frank Nash, a federal prisoner, who had escaped from the U.S. Penitentiary at Leavenworth, Kansas, and had been recently apprehended. In the exchange of gunfire, four law enforcement officers and Nash were killed. An intensive search by the FBI and local authorities culminated on October 22, 1934, when Floyd was killed in a shoot-out on an Ohio farm field with federal agents and local police. Cadet Hall, who had had his own brushes with the law, was a student at Kemper Military School at the time of that bloody denouement, soon to achieve legendary status in criminal lore. Hall's own cold-blooded behaviour was to reach full flower only a few years later—aided, perhaps, by the mystique of role models like Floyd, who was surely the talk of the schoolyard.

Hall soon gained a reputation as a well-dressed, devil-may-care ladies' man who sported a thin moustache, spent his money freely, and gambled on the horses. In 1946, he ran off with a married Pleasanton woman named Irene Holmes, and after her divorce came through they were married in the spa town of Excelsior

Springs, Missouri. He also purchased a home at 818 West 59th Street Terrace just off fashionable Ward Parkway in Kansas City, Missouri, near the Missouri-Kansas state line.

"I hate little people," Hall once boasted. "I like to be big."

Mission Hills, Kansas, where the Greenleases and other wealthy Kansas Citians lived, was virtually within walking distance. An affluent suburb of Kansas City, Missouri, which lay to the east, Mission Hills had been founded in the early 1900s as America's first garden community by urban planner J. C. Nichols, who also developed Kansas City's renowned Country Club Plaza. Set amid wooded hills and winding streams, the exclusive enclave where the Greenleases lived was also surrounded by a green belt of three golf courses, and the public areas were adorned with fountains, sculptures, and urns. Hall almost certainly drove or walked through the suburb while shopping for a home of his own, or to check out where his former classmate, Paul Greenlease, had lived as a boy; and the sumptuousness of the homes could only have fed his envy. Even with his substantial inheritance, he did not have the deep pockets necessary to belong to one of America's wealthiest communities.

From time to time, Hall liked to return to Pleasanton, driving his Cadillac convertible and often in the company of men he liked to introduce as "my broker" and "my lawyer."

A year after his marriage, Hall went into partnership with another man, Buzz Herschfield, in a crop dusting scheme. They purchased two small prop planes, hired two pilots, and managed to secure a few contracts, but crop spraying that year was hampered by heavy rains. Enterprisingly, they then obtained a government contract to spray mosquitoes in rain-swollen backwaters. But after one of the planes crashed, Hall quit the venture. His losses were later variously estimated at from $4,000 to $18,000.

Undeterred, in 1948 Hall bought a new Buick and drove to California to pursue another business venture. He was accompanied by a friend who had some affairs of his own to look after, and went along for the ride. After the pair checked into a Los Angeles hotel, Hall simply disappeared for two weeks. The two men then drove back to Kansas City, stopping in Las Vegas along the way, where Hall won $1,500 at the craps table. He also bought a new Cadillac, though records showed that it was not purchased from the Greenlease Motor Company or any other Kansas City dealer.

Other ventures soon followed: a plan to pipe music into hospitals and sell earphones to patients; and two liquor stores in Bates County, Missouri, not far from Pleasanton.

Oppressed by Hall's heavy drinking, Irene divorced him while he was in California in 1950. They had no children. She left him just before his money ran out. He had squandered his entire inheritance, mostly on drink and gambling, in less than five years.

On May 14, 1951, broke and desperate, Hall was arrested in Milwaukee for trying to sell a 1948 Oldsmobile without revealing to the prospective buyer that the car had a lien on it. He was charged with vagrancy, but after he returned the money the case was dismissed.

Sometime later he robbed a store in Kingman, Kansas, but charges were dropped after he was arrested a third time in Kansas City. With his last $20, he had bought a pistol and started robbing cabs. On September 16 of that year, police charged him with holding up eight cabdrivers. In each case, he politely displayed his gun to the driver, assuring him that he would not be hurt if he handed over the money. He was finally caught after stealing $10 from a cabbie, and then taking the cab. The police arrested him after a brief chase. When Hall reached for his pistol, patrolman William Peters knocked him down with a blow to the jaw. The series of thefts had brought him a grand haul of just $33.

Hall later confessed that he had previously cased the Plaza Bank of Commerce, and had gone back the next day—the day of his arrest—to rob it, only to discover to his dismay that it was closed on Saturdays. He was found guilty and sentenced to five years in the Missouri State Penitentiary in Jefferson City. He remained there for a year and three months, and was paroled on April 24, 1953.

During his stay in prison, Hall worked as a nurse and began reading medical textbooks. While lying on his bunk bed, he also fantasized about how to pull off a kidnapping, which he considered the easiest way to become wealthy again. He knew that the family of Paul Greenlease, his former classmate at Kemper Military School, was worth millions. Somewhere along the line—probably from reading newspaper accounts about Paul's father, a respected community business leader and owner of several Cadillac dealerships—he also learned that the older Greenlease and his young wife were the parents of two school-age children. The Greenlease family seemed like a ready-made answer to his prayers.

The hospital dispensary gave Hall access not only to drugs, but also to textbooks that contained information a man contemplating murder might find useful—how quickly a body decomposes, for example. He later invited a cellmate to join him, but the convict declined.

"I'll be driving Cadillacs when you're carrying a lunch basket," Hall sneered. Cadillacs lately were much on his mind.

Upon his parole, Hall went to St. Joseph, Missouri, where a local attorney, Bernard ("Barney") Patton, found him a job as an automobile salesman. Patton had formerly done some legal work for Hall during several of his business ventures, and also helped secure his early release from prison. A chronic failure at just about everything he tried, Hall worked at several car dealerships in St. Joseph before he was fired for drinking. Patton then helped get him a job as an insurance salesman. Though Hall was not successful in that line of work either, he did manage to sell at least one policy—to a woman named Bonnie Brown Heady.

Hall and Heady met in the latter part of May 1953, about a month after he was released from prison, at the Pony Express bar of the Hotel Robidoux in downtown St. Joseph. The hotel was the city's finest. Its bar—decorated in a Scottish tartan motif—was a popular gathering place, and its dining room similarly enjoyed a reputation as St. Joseph's best.

Born on July 15, 1912, on a farm in Burlington Junction, Missouri, Bonnie Emily Brown was the daughter of French P. Brown, a prosperous farmer, and Mabel Clutter Brown. Her mother died when Bonnie turned two, and she was mostly raised by her maternal aunt and uncle, Nellie and Ed Clutter, who were sister and brother. Bonnie attended church as a child. Her former second-grade schoolteacher at the Hazel Dell school in Clearmont, Missouri, near the Iowa border, remembered her as a quiet, obedient girl with long black curls. During Bonnie's high school years, Nellie often drove her niece into town to attend a basketball game, or a school party, and then waited for her in a Model T roadster. While attending Clearmont High School, Bonnie made the honours list in 1931, the year she graduated.

Like Hall, Bonnie enrolled in college after high school—in her case, Northwest Missouri State College in Maryville—and, like him, dropped out after only a few months. After taking a hairdresser's course, she went to work in a beauty salon, and in June 1932, at the age of twenty, she married Vernon Ellis Heady, who became a successful livestock merchant. Among the couple's pastimes were going to square dances, and showing and breeding pedigree boxers. Heady also became an accomplished horsewoman, and often rode her favourite palomino mare in parades on public holidays.

The Headys lived comfortably in a six-room, white-frame bungalow in St. Joseph that reflected the tastes of a well-to-do suburban couple—bookshelves stacked with about two hundred bestsellers and detective novels; dozens of figurines and bric-a-brac; trophies won by Heady's boxers. The dining room was furnished with an antique dresser; and a flattering charcoal drawing of a younger Heady, dated 1941, hung on a wall. The closets were jam-packed with hundreds of dresses, and her dressing table was crowded with thirty-five perfume bottles and nearly one hundred pieces of costume jewellery.

But the marriage was childless—due to Vernon Heady's brutal insistence that Bonnie have eleven illegal abortions because he did not want children. Bonnie once confided to a friend that she had wanted children in the early years of her marriage, but later began to dislike them intensely.

In 1948, Heady's father died and she inherited $44,000 and a 316-acre farm north of Maryville from his estate. By then, her marriage had broken down, and she mostly preferred to stay at home alone, drinking. Apparently, during this time, she also suffered a mental breakdown. Occasionally, she showed up drunk at a dog show. Once, she cursed a neighbour for allowing a dog to enter her well-tended back yard. In a 1951 competition, she won third prize as best-dressed cowgirl.

In September 1952, Heady sued for divorce on grounds of adultery, alleging that her husband left home for long periods of time and refused to say where he was going, or where he had been. In her presence, she further claimed, he was "sullen and morose." When the divorce was granted the following month, she received the couple's blue-shuttered house at 1201 South 38th Street in the settlement. Soon afterwards a strange man moved in with her. Neighbours began to complain of loud parties and suspicious-looking visitors. The local sheriff's office twice sent deputies to investigate disturbances.

Heady and her male companion also remodelled a spare bedroom on the second floor into a dimly lit barroom, replete with a cabinet well stocked with Old Stagg whisky, photographs and four large posters of nude women on the walls, a slot machine, a phonograph player and records, and, incongruously, a bookcase containing a complete set of the *World Book* encyclopedia. A large partitioned closet off the second floor contained the overflow of the four downstairs closets—even more expensive women's clothing. A woman friend who had become disgusted with Heady's behaviour and had stopped seeing her, maintaining a tenuous relationship only by telephone, later recalled, "She had enough clothes to last a normal woman twenty-five years." All had been bought at exclusive women's shops in a variety of cities.

As she grew older and her youthful appearance faded, Heady craved more and more clothing. Soon the money to buy it ran out, and there was scarcely enough to pay the utility bills. That was when she turned, as her erstwhile friend delicately phrased it, "to other ways of getting money." Working as a prostitute out of her own home—even though she received rental income from her farm—Heady paid cabdrivers a $2 fee for each referral. She later estimated that she serviced about 150 men, charging $20 a trick. Occasionally, she also posed with another woman for pornographic photos.

On the morning of May 20, 1953, around the time she met Hall, Heady hired Maxine Richardson as a cleaning woman. Three hours later, while she was in the back yard burning trash, Richardson heard gunfire, went inside, and found a man lying in the middle of the floor, bleeding. Richardson got her coat and left. Local police soon arrived. Heady had shot the man, a travelling salesman from Maryville, where she still owned a farm, in the wrist. Both Heady and the man—a customer—had been drinking, and he had tried several times to extinguish a lit cigarette on her breasts. He declined to prosecute.

Heady's favourite place to pick up customers was the Pony Express bar, and at first Hall was just one more in a very long line. And yet he was a little different from the others, too. On the day they met, Hall spent the night at Heady's home. Just two days later, they began living as husband and wife. Hall told Heady that he was an ex-convict on parole from the Missouri State Penitentiary, but did not initially tell her that he had been convicted of armed robbery. He said that he had been imprisoned for insurance fraud.

He wasted little time taking over as Heady's pimp. His endearment for her was "Baby doll," and she called him "Honey bunch."

What kept them together was not mutual sexual attraction, since Hall continued to market Heady—his only capital—to potential johns. Yet Heady's degradation and debasement only served to increase her emotional dependence on her new protector, pimp, and lover. She had reached rock bottom from a high place, and had no one else to turn to.

Hall, too, had run out of options, schemes, and daydreams—except for the one last long shot he had fantasized about while lying on his prison bunk bed. A not particularly discriminating user of other people, he saw in Heady the one indispensable ingredient he needed to make his grand kidnapping plan work—a pliable accomplice. Even though he needed her, he beat her regularly, but she always forgave him and took him back. Their common bond was whisky. They also shared a near-hopeless mutual desperation, and such sociopathic or psychopathic indicators—particularly in Hall's case—as chronic lying, an inability to feel remorse, frequent trouble with the law, extreme moodiness, paranoia, and so on, down a very long list.

Sometime in mid-June, after Hall had taken Heady's measure, he revealed to her his plan to perpetrate a kidnapping. It was the one foolproof method, he explained, for obtaining a large amount of money quickly with a minimal chance of being detected. He also confided that the victim would be either the daughter or son of Robert C. Greenlease, a wealthy local automobile dealer.

At first, Heady dismissed the scheme as mere talk. But soon enough she came under the spell of his obsession, and what especially bewitched her was that he genuinely wanted her to be a part of his plan. He also promised to exonerate her of all blame if they were apprehended. Her ostensible cover story was that Hall had lied to her, telling her that the kidnapped child was his own from a previous marriage. Heady, as hard-bitten as Hall, did not require much persuasion. She was willing to do anything to keep him.

What Hall did not reveal in their early planning stages was that he intended to murder his victim. Nor did he suggest that the child, after he or she was murdered, might have to be buried in Heady's back yard. He only boasted that Greenlease was a man of considerable wealth, and that "I intend to get a lot of it."

In several phone calls to the Greenlease residence in Mission Hills, Heady—posing as a school official—talked to the maid, who told her the names and ages of the Greenlease children, what schools they attended, and other relevant information, including the fact that Bobby owned a pet parrot. Heady also learned that the family was vacationing in Europe until early September when school started for Bobby and his older sister, Virginia Sue.

On August 28, Hall took Heady's station wagon to the Donaldson Radio and Electric Company in Kansas City and had a shortwave converter installed in the radio that made it possible for him to overhear police communications.

Early one September morning, two weeks before the kidnapping was actually to take place, Hall and Heady drove to the Greenleases' ivy-fringed residence in Mission Hills and trailed the children's father as he chauffeured them to school. They took careful note of the time he left the family home, and what time he dropped the boy off at the French Institute.

Hall even considered going to the Greenlease mansion—after ascertaining that Bobby's father was at work and his mother away on an errand—and simply abducting the boy. He also still wondered whether he should abduct Virginia Sue instead. In fact, he nearly did seize the Greenleases' daughter off a Kansas City street. Two weeks prior to the kidnapping, he and Heady tailed Virginia Greenlease as she picked up Virginia Sue at her school, and then drove to Country Club Plaza. After parking her Cadillac, Mrs. Greenlease entered a nearby drugstore. Possessed by a sudden urge, Hall got out of the station wagon and hurried over to the car, hoping to simply grab the girl as she waited for her mother to return. Instead, he saw that eleven-year-old Virginia Sue was, in fact, opening the car door to join her mother—and, furthermore, that she was much older and more mature than he had assumed from his earlier scouting expeditions. Then and there, he determined to kidnap the Greenleases' younger and presumably much more malleable son.

As Hall and Heady continued to monitor the schedules of Bobby's mother and father in the days leading up to the kidnapping, Hall mentioned more than once how incriminating it would be for the two kidnappers if Bobby could identify them after his release. The need to dispose of the boy soon after he was abducted was an insistent drumbeat in his conversation. "He's evidence," Hall warned her, again and again. By now, Heady had upped her whisky consumption to two fifths a day, and was seldom if ever sober. She would later claim that she did not finally agree to murdering Bobby until the morning of September 27, the day before the actual kidnapping. But so many of Hall's preparations laid the groundwork for both killing Bobby and disposing of his body that either she was simply dissembling, or more likely lost in such an alcoholic fog that she no longer knew or remembered what she had agreed to. Regardless, Hall had no doubt that, when the time came, he would prevail. Two other characteristics of the psychopath, which Hall had in spades, were deceitfulness and an ability to smoothly manipulate people. Heady never stood a chance.

To predispose and accustom her to the idea of killing Bobby, Hall sometimes liked to discuss the different ways a body could be hidden—all "hypothetically," of course. One was to drop it into the Missouri River. The problem with that scenario was that the boy's corpse might eventually float to the surface. As Hall reminded Heady again and again, the Greenlease family needed to believe during ransom negotiations that their boy was still alive.

He also suggested burying Bobby in a wood on the Kansas side of the state line. But when he took her to see the spot he was thinking of, bulldozers were already there, turning up earth, apparently preparing the land for a subdivision.

On September 10—in a clear indication that Hall already had every intention of murdering Bobby soon after he was kidnapped— he bought a fifty-pound bag of Ash Grove Veri-Fat lime for eighty-five cents from the Sawyer Material Company in Kansas City, and hauled it into Heady's basement. Somewhere he had read that hot lime dissolved human flesh and bone.

Hall's other purchases included a .38 calibre Smith & Wesson revolver—a so-called banker's special; a holster; and a box of cartridges from Uncle Sam's Loan Office, a pawnshop located on Minnesota Avenue in Kansas City, Kansas. He also bought some ammunition for a .25 calibre revolver Heady owned—the same one she had used to shoot the john in the wrist some months earlier.

At a variety store in St. Joseph, Hall bought a pad of Hytone linen-finish stationery, for writing the ransom note. At a post office, he picked up some prepaid envelopes. By now he had decided on the amount of the ransom—$600,000, by far the largest ransom ever to be paid in America. In today's money, that amount would be the equivalent of about $10 million.*

---

*In 1968, kidnapper Gary Krist abducted Barbara Jane Mackle and buried her in a box near Atlanta, Georgia. She was freed after the family paid $500,000 in ransom. Krist was captured and sentenced to life in prison. In 1974, ex-convict William A. H. Williams and his wife, Betty Ruth, kidnapped Reg Murphy, an editorial writer for *The Atlanta Constitution*. Murphy was freed after the newspaper paid a $700,000 ransom. Williams was captured and given a forty-year sentence; his wife received a three-year suspended sentence.

In Rome in 1973, the family of J. Paul Getty paid kidnappers $2.9 million to ransom sixteen-year-old J. Paul Getty III, whose right ear had been sent to his family during his captivity. His kidnappers were never caught. The following year, Exxon paid $14.2 million to Marxist guerrillas in Argentina for the return of Victor Samuelson, manager of Esso Argentina. In 1975, the Bulgari family in Italy paid $16 million in ransom for the release of jeweller Giovanni Bulgari. He was released in Rome, and his kidnappers were never apprehended. Samuel Bronfman II, heir to the Seagram liquor fortune, was kidnapped in New York in 1976. The family paid a ransom of $2.3 million. The chief kidnapper turned out to be the young man's homosexual lover. The kidnappers said young Bronfman had blackmailed them into the hoax as a way to extort money from his father. They were found innocent of kidnapping, but guilty of extortion.

Hall had settled on that figure because he once read a magazine article that gave the weight and size of a package containing a million dollars in $10 and $20 denominations. A million dollars, he figured, would simply be both too bulky and too heavy. But $600,000 stashed in a large duffel bag would weigh between eighty and eighty-five pounds, and not be too unwieldy for a man of his size to handle without drawing attention to himself.

Hall also guessed that, after the payment of the ransom became public, the serial numbers of the currency would be published. If all the bills came from the same Federal Reserve bank, that would make it too easy for the authorities to keep track of the serial numbers of any ransom money being spent. Hall resolved that the ransom therefore had to be collected from all twelve Federal Reserve banks to confound law enforcement agencies.

Finally, Hall bought Bobby's shroud, a blue plastic sheet to wrap around his victim before he placed the boy in his grave, at a Western Auto Supply in St. Joseph. He also guessed that the ransom might be treated with a chemical or powder to identify him as the kidnapper by staining his hands or clothing. To circumvent that possibility, he bought two additional blue plastic sheets, which he planned to wrap around the duffel bag filled with money, and so make his escape undetected.

One evening, just prior to the kidnapping, Hall and Heady went to a bar in Riverside, a Kansas City suburb, and Hall got quite drunk. As they drove home, with Hall at the wheel, they had a minor traffic accident. Though a fender on Heady's car was dented, the other car did not stop, and no report of the accident was made. But Heady insisted on driving home the rest of the way. En route to St. Joseph, Hall rolled down the window of the station wagon and fired a shot from his revolver into the night sky.

Just before the kidnapping, the pair also drove to downtown Kansas City, where Hall bought a copy of *The Daily Oklahoman*, an Oklahoma City newspaper, at Ruback's, a newsstand near the Muehlebach Hotel. Hall knew that Mr. Greenlease owned an interest in an Oklahoma City automobile dealership, and wanted to make use of a Greenlease-O'Neill Oldsmobile advertisement when he mailed the first ransom letter to the Greenlease home. That tactic, he hoped, would deceive the authorities into thinking that the kidnappers were based in Oklahoma. After finding the newspaper advertisement, he clipped it, and later cut out the name "Greenlease" and pasted it on an envelope.

Around 4 P.M. on Saturday, September 26, two days before the kidnapping, he also bought a long-handled True Temper shovel from the Hatfield Hardware Company in St. Joseph. Grace Hatfield, who waited on him, asked what kind of shovel he was looking for.

"It don't make any difference what kind of shovel," he told her. "I'm only going to use it once anyway."

On Sunday, the day before the kidnapping, Hall stole a pair of Missouri licence plates in St. Joseph and put them on Heady's station wagon. He also used his long-handled shovel to dig the grave near the back porch. Badly out of shape, he perspired profusely and stopped frequently to go inside to rest and have a drink. Finally, he finished. The grave measured three feet deep by five feet long.

Before the day was over, and after the grave had been dug, Hall also composed the first ransom letter. While Heady printed it out, Hall repeatedly corrected her spelling. Once they were finished, he placed the note in the envelope on which he had pasted the name "Greenlease," and put that envelope into a large prepaid envelope addressed to "Robert C. Greenlease, 2600 Verowa Rd., Kansas City, Mo."

Despite all of his careful planning, and even having driven past the Greenlease house as part of his surveillance, Hall managed to put the wrong address on his ransom demand. The Greenleases lived at 2920 Verona Road, and their home was located in Mission Hills, Kansas, not in Kansas City, Missouri.

Robert Cosgrove Greenlease, Bobby's father, was born in 1882 on a farm in Saline County in west-central Missouri. In 1894, when Robert was twelve, the family moved to Kansas City. Around the turn of the century, the horse and buggy was being replaced by automobiles; and in 1903, when he was nearly twenty-one, Greenlease and a partner set up a small shop and began manufacturing and selling a three-cylinder car called the Kansas City Hummer with "a copper water jacket" and no top. Handmade like all cars in those pre–assembly line days, it sold for $3,300. After building four automobiles, the two young men abandoned the enterprise. Greenlease set up an auto repair garage, but soon got back into the retail business, trying to sell the legendary Thomas Flyer, a car that had crossed Siberia to win a New York–to–Paris race.

In 1908, Greenlease obtained a franchise to sell Cadillac automobiles. Soon afterwards, General Motors bought the company and business prospered. He also sold Oldsmobiles, and in time became the largest distributor of Cadillacs in the Southwest in a territory ranging from the Texas panhandle to Colorado. In addition, he was a partner in dealerships in Topeka, Kansas; Tulsa, Oklahoma; and other cities. Under a contract negotiated with Cadillac Motors before it was absorbed by General Motors, he also earned a commission on every Cadillac sold by other dealers in Missouri, Kansas, Oklahoma, and parts of Iowa and Nebraska. By the 1950s he was said to be one of the ten wealthiest men in Kansas City, and he was also allegedly one of the largest stockholders in General Motors. (Hall later claimed that he had checked with Dun & Bradstreet and found that Robert Greenlease was worth $24 million, or the equivalent of more than $350 million today.)

Greenlease and his first wife had no children but adopted a boy, Paul Robert Greenlease. In 1939 the couple divorced. When he reached high school age, Paul was sent to the Kemper Military School in Boonville, a military academy that specialized in educating children with disciplinary problems.

Also in 1939, just months after his divorce, the fifty-eight-year-old Robert Greenlease married Virginia Pollock, a woman exactly half his age. Virginia Greenlease was a Kansas City native and a graduate of the Research School of Nursing. In 1941 she gave birth to a daughter, Virginia Sue, and in 1947 a son, Robert Cosgrove Greenlease, Jr. The boy's father was sixty-five when his son was born. Virginia was thirty-eight.

Little Bobby was doted on. He had his own miniature motorized Cadillac, two dogs, and a green parrot. The family lived in a sumptuous Tudor-style mansion in Mission Hills. Among the servants were a housekeeper, a gardener/handyman, a Swedish maid, and Bobby's governess. In the summer of 1953, only months before the kidnapping, the family toured Europe, taking the governess with them.

Virginia Sue Greenlease was enrolled in a fashionable girls school in Sunset Hill, and Bobby attended the French Institute of Notre Dame de Sion, an exclusive elementary school in Kansas City run by the Sisters of Sion, a French order of nuns.

After Mère Marthanna called the Greenlease home Monday morning, September 28, to inquire about Mrs. Greenlease's condition, Virginia Greenlease immediately hung up and called her husband, and he in turn called the police, asking that Chief Bernard C. Brannon meet him at 29th Street and the McGee trafficway. He then informed Brannon of what had happened and asked the police chief to accompany him home.

Two detectives, Harry Nesbitt and Richard Bennett, soon arrived at the Greenlease home to interview Bobby's parents.

Early in the afternoon, Virginia Greenlease collapsed under the strain and was given a sedative. Her husband showed emotion only once. When he met a close friend of the family at the front door, she embraced him and said, "Oh, Bob. It just can't be true, can it?"

"Yes, it is," he replied. But his jaw trembled, tears filled his eyes, and he was unable to continue.

Virginia Sue, like her mother, cried almost continuously during the afternoon after she was brought home from school. Much of the time, she simply followed her father around the house, tears in her eyes.

At first, the police delayed making any announcement in the hope that Bobby might be found. But at 3 P.M. the police officially announced that there had been a kidnapping. Many of the Greenleases' friends called or went directly to their home, offering any assistance that might be needed. Chief Brannon promised to take personal charge of the case. The police were also working closely with Wesley Grapp, the assistant special agent in charge of the local office of the Federal Bureau of Investigation. In a reference to the Lindbergh Law, Grapp told reporters that he was waiting to see if any developments indicated a violation of a federal statute. The Lindbergh Law declared that transportation of a kidnapped person across a state line or into a foreign country was a federal offence. In Missouri, kidnapping for ransom was punishable by imprisonment or death.

At 6 P.M., Robert and Virginia Sue Greenlease sat in the living room to watch a news report on television about the kidnapping. They were joined by Stewart M. Johnson, general manager of the Greenlease firm; Elsie Utlaut, the children's governess; and Britt Selander, a maid. During the newscast, Willard Creech, the taxi driver who had delivered Heady and Bobby to the Katz Drug Store parking lot, told an interviewer that the woman had asked about Bobby's black parrot.

"The parrot isn't black," Virginia Sue interjected. "Green."

During the remainder of the evening, Johnson and Norbert S. O'Neill, partner with Greenlease in Greenlease-O'Neill Oldsmobile, took telephone messages.

2.

The Vigil

On the drive back to Kansas City, Hall took a new highway that Heady did not recognize, and eventually crossed into North Kansas City by way of the airport bridge. They then stopped for a second time at Lynn's Tavern, where earlier that morning they had fortified their nerves with several shots of whisky. Pulling into a rear parking lot, Hall switched the licence plates once again, reattaching the originals. While he was changing plates, Heady entered the bar and had two drinks, and also took at least one out to Hall, who was inspecting the car to make sure no blood was dripping from the back end. Since Hall's clothes were splattered with blood, he did not want to go into the bar. They then drove directly to St. Joseph.

Once home, Hall pulled into the basement garage. Heady entered through the front door of the house and unlocked the door at the top of the basement steps so that Hall could bring the body through the kitchen, onto the back porch, and into the yard. Before burying Bobby, Hall removed the Jerusalem medal from the boy's shirt. He made several trips back and forth, getting the lime and tools ready, while Heady steadied herself with another two or three drinks.

The last time that Heady glimpsed the body, it was lying in the grave. Hall had already thrown the lime over Bobby's remains and begun to fill in the dirt. When he was half-finished, he went down to the garage and washed out the back of the station wagon with a hose. Eager to post the ransom letter before the last mail pick up of the day, he informed Heady that he had to hurry into Kansas City, and instructed her to finish burying Bobby. Using a hose, a shovel, and an axe, she continued to add dirt until it was within about a half-foot of ground level.

She was still fussing about the grave when Hall called collect from a drugstore at 31st Street and Main in Kansas City to tell her that everything was proceeding according to plan, and urged her not to worry. He had dropped the letter to the Greenleases in a mailbox on the corner of 39th Street and Broadway. He then returned to St. Joseph, stopping along the way for a few drinks. Back home, he resumed cleaning the basement with turpentine, gasoline, water, and other materials, using a broom to scrub away the bloodstains. He also threw the empty shells from his .38 calibre revolver into a wastebasket, and later tossed its contents into an incinerator.

Hall also took his suit to Hodson Cleaners, explaining to the clerk that the bloodstains were the result of an accident. He put his bloodied shirt into the washing machine at Heady's home.

In the evening, the two kidnappers stayed home, drinking heavily and watching television. A flood tide of whisky had transported them across a profound human divide. They had no compass, moral or otherwise, to guide them now, and their only certainty was that a murdered child lay buried in their back yard.

Just nine hours after Bobby was taken from his school, Hall's incorrectly addressed ransom letter, postmarked 6 P.M. on September 28 and sent Special Delivery, arrived at the Greenlease home. The police had alerted the Postal Service to be on the lookout for any mail addressed to the family. The badly misspelled letter read:

Your boy has been kiddnapped get $600,000 in $20s—$10s— Fed. Res. Notes from all twelve districts we realize it takes a few days to get that amount. Boy will be in good hands— when you have money ready put ad in K.C. Star. M—will meet you this week in Chicago—signed Mr. G.

Do not call police or try to use chemicals on bills or take numbers. Do not try to use any radio to catch us or boy dies. If you try to trap us your wife and your other child and yourself will be killed you will be watched all of the time. You will be told later how to contact us with money. When you get this note let us know by driving up an down main St. between 29 & 39 for twenty minutes with white rag on car aeriel.

The ransom note continued on the other side:

If do exactly as we say an try no tricks, your boy will be back safe withen 24 hrs afer we check money.

Deliver money in army duefel bag. Be ready to deliver at once on contact.

M.
$400,000 in 20s
$200,000 in 10s.

Hall had chosen to sign his ransom demand with the letter "M," but it held no special significance. As he later noted, "I could just as well have used any other letter of the alphabet."

On Tuesday morning, September 29, Hall continued to clean up the basement. Heady, suffering from a severe hangover, did not join him. As he continued to mentally replay all that had happened, a badly hungover Hall finally realized that he had mailed the first ransom demand to the wrong address. With Heady's help, he then drafted a second ransom letter, reiterating the demands set forth in the first, and enclosing the Jerusalem medal that he had taken from Bobby's body. The pair then proceeded to the McIninch Florist Shop on a parkway outside St. Joseph and bought a dozen chrysanthemum plants. Returning home, they planted the flowers in the newly turned earth, and watered them.

Later that day, Hall and Heady drove to Kansas City, stopping as usual at Lynn's for a few drinks prior to mailing the second letter—this time with the correct address—at the main post office downtown. It was postmarked 9:30 P.M. Hall also called the Greenlease home to ask two questions: "Did you get my note?" "Are you preparing the money?" Greenlease business associate Stewart Johnson assured him that the answer to both was in the affirmative. When Hall complained that he had not seen a car drive along the designated route with a white rag on its aerial, Johnson insisted that the trip had nevertheless been made. Since the Greenlease family was already receiving a number of crank calls, the two men also agreed that henceforth all conversations between the family and Hall would follow a strict formula. Hall would be asked to identify himself, and he would reply, "M. Ribbon," a reference to the ribbon on Bobby's Jerusalem medal.

Returning home late in the evening, Hall and Heady again both got very drunk.

Again thanks to an alert Postal Service, the second letter was delivered to the Greenlease home early Wednesday morning. The hastily composed abbreviated note read:

You must not of got our first letter. Show this to no one. Get $600,000 in 10$ and 20$ federal reserve notes from all distrisst 400,000 in 20s—200,000—10s you will not take numbers or treat bills in any way. When you have money put ad in star personal will meet you in Chicago Sunday G. Call police off and obey instructions Boy is ok but homesick. Don't try to stop us or pick up or boy dies you will hear from us later. Put money in army duffle bag.

Since this letter contained Bobby's Jerusalem medal, the Greenlease family was now convinced they were dealing with the real kidnappers.

Visibly distraught, Robert Greenlease appeared in front of his house to speak to the small army of reporters camped outside. "We think they are trying to make contact," he said, sobbing. "All I want is my boy back."

The Greenlease family now decided to form a three-man telephone committee to serve on a twenty-four-hour basis. Comprising the group were Bobby's stepbrother Paul Greenlease, Johnson, and Norbert O'Neill. The group agreed that Johnson would not personally answer the phone because the kidnappers might confuse him with Henry W. Johnson, a former Kansas City police chief who currently served as superintendent of traffic. Robert L. Ledterman, also a close friend and business associate, served as family spokesman.

Immediately after receiving the second ransom letter, Robert Greenlease consulted with Ledterman, O'Neill, Johnson, and his family, and decided to comply with its demands. Ledterman contacted Arthur B. Eisenhower, brother of President Dwight D. Eisenhower and president of the Commerce Trust Company in Kansas City. Eisenhower called H. Gavin Leedy, president of the Kansas City branch of the Federal Reserve Bank, who ordered that the $600,000 ransom be amassed in the strictest secrecy from all twelve Federal Reserve banks. Eighty clerks worked throughout the night to assemble the forty thousand separate pieces of currency. The money remained sacked in the bank from the morning of Wednesday, September 30, until 5 P.M. Saturday,

October 3, when Ledterman and Robert T. Moore, an Oklahoma City automobile dealer and Greenlease associate, collected it.

Ledterman also placed a classified advertisement in *The Kansas City Star*, indicating as directed that the ransom money had been assembled.

The *Star* first reported the story with a brief item in its afternoon edition on Monday, September 28, the very day of the kidnapping, noting only that an unidentified woman had taken Bobby Greenlease from the French Institute of Notre Dame de Sion.

The next day, the kidnapping made front-page news when the newspaper ran a story under a three-column headline: "Child Kidnaped on a Ruse. Woman Pretending to Be an Aunt of Robert C. Greenlease, Jr., 6, Takes Him from the French Institute of Notre Dame de Sion, 3823 Locust." Heady was described as "35 or 40 years old, about 5 feet 5 inches tall, weighing about 135 pounds, chunky build, reddish hair, wearing a white blouse, dark brown skirt."

The paper also reported that a housekeeper at the Greenlease home recalled that, about ten days earlier, she had received a telephone call from a woman who said she was a representative from the public schools, and wanted to know the ages of the children in the family, and where they attended class. Public school officials denied conducting any such survey.

Cab driver Willard Creech was quoted as saying that, when he left Bobby and the mystery woman at the Katz parking lot, they headed toward a blue Ford that was either a 1952 or a 1953 model. (Heady's car was a 1951 Plymouth.) But he was unable to continue observing them because just then a car honked behind him, and he was forced to move out of the way. The nuns at the school confirmed that Bobby showed no fear when he left the school in the woman's company.

The *St. Louis Post-Dispatch* did not run an item on the kidnapping and ransom demand until Wednesday, September 30, and even then relegated it to page 37. Front-page news in St. Louis included a story about the sale of the St. Louis Browns, the city's cellar-dwelling American League baseball franchise, to a Baltimore syndicate for $2,475,000; and an item about the record-breaking 101-degree temperature on the previous afternoon. In other news, the first game of the World Series was scheduled to begin at Yankee Stadium, with the Bronx Bombers playing host to the Brooklyn Dodgers.

The days passed grimly at the Greenlease home. Bobby's father at first held out hope that the kidnapping was the work of professionals, who presumably would be interested primarily in collecting a ransom and less likely to harm the child. Neither parent was able to sleep, except for brief naps. "About all we can do is sit and wring our hands and hope," Greenlease told reporters. A local truck driver reported seeing a man, a woman, and a child who fit the descriptions of Bobby and his abductors in a red pick up soon after Heady left the school with the boy. Others called from as far away as Boston, Chicago, and New York. At Notre Dame de Sion, the 220 pupils took turns filing into the chapel in groups to pray for Bobby's safe return. The public was also urged to be on the lookout for a six-year-old boy who stood about thirty-eight to forty inches tall, weighed about fifty-three pounds, whose lower left front tooth was missing. He was last seen wearing a white short-sleeved shirt, short brown linen trousers, dark brown socks, and brown leather shoes with a white leather tongue. Pinned to his shirt was a small bronze school medal with a red ribbon. The authorities included this last item in their description of Bobby, even though the medal had already been returned to the boy's family, because the Greenleases felt that secrecy was essential in their negotiations with the kidnappers, and they did not want to make any information public.

Forty-eight hours after Bobby was taken, the police closed the

Greenlease home to visitors. Both parents remained in seclusion, with Virginia Greenlease under the watchful care of a physician. Unaware that the kidnappers had almost immediately contacted the family, the press remained as much in the dark as the public, and continued to report that the kidnappers' silence only deepened the mystery of who had taken little Bobby. Police officials admitted that their investigation had already reached an impasse. Another hypothesis now being considered was that perhaps a woman who was mentally disturbed had taken Bobby. Police quickly discounted the theory that professionals had taken Bobby, since the woman who showed up at the school could be readily identified if she appeared in public. Robert Greenlease now hoped that the kidnapping was the work of a hoodlum interested only in money, because that meant Bobby would be released when payment was made.

On Wednesday morning, two days after Bobby vanished, Ledterman drove Virginia Greenlease to mass. He, Johnson, and other Greenlease associates and friends were concerned not only for her health, but also for Robert's, as he was now seventy-one and the strain was increasingly intense. Paul Greenlease arrived early each morning, as usual, to be with his father. By now reporters were calling from St. Louis, Chicago, Philadelphia, and numerous other cities, and in each case Ledterman's response was the same: There was nothing new to report. Eugene Pond, chief of detectives, stated that the police were no nearer to a solution, and FBI agents publicly said that they would not become officially involved until the parents received some demand for a ransom—although, of course, two had already been received.

Later that same Wednesday, Ledterman—a genial, heavyset man who always dressed in a white shirt and dark tie—told reporters: "We have received about eight telephone calls during the day from cranks who say they have the child. I talk to the persons making the calls and ask them questions about the appearance of the boy or what he was wearing. That ends the conversation because they don't know the answers. On several occasions the telephone rang and there would be nobody at the other end when you answered."

Two nuns from Notre Dame de Sion visited the home on Wednesday afternoon, staying about an hour. The Greenlease home also became a popular destination for sightseers eager to see the scene of such national excitement.

The papers further reported that a considerable number of people had phoned police headquarters to say that they, too, had received calls from someone asking about the number of children in their home, their names and ages, and where they attended school. Police learned that a company trying to sell encyclopaedia sets was making the calls, and it agreed to stop.

Heady, meanwhile, continued to live in a world that was half-fantasy and half-delusion. Around noon on Wednesday, September 30, she applied for a $10,000 loan at the Drovers and Merchants Bank in St. Joseph, using her 316 acre farm as security. Her intention was to pay her former husband $2,000 as a final settlement in their divorce, which became official at the end of October; and also to repay a $2,000 loan to the bank that fell due in January 1954. Some of the money would also be used to pay for a new hardtop Studebaker convertible that she had ordered from Carnes Motor Company, a local agency. The car was scheduled to be delivered on October 13. The balance of the loan would be used to pay for her and Hall's travelling expenses to what she called "Old Mexico" until they could safely live a life of luxury in La Jolla. An updated version of their fantasies now called for them to invest in a motel that they would manage together. Both still agreed, though, that they would never be away during the winter thoroughbred racing season. They also planned to be married in Chicago the week of October 12.

That same day, mindful that she and Hall were still on a budget, Heady also returned several items to Bruns' Hy-Klas Food Store and got a refund of $1.29.

Never once did she and Hall discuss dividing the money between them, or of separating and going their different ways after the kidnapping. In fact, Heady had suggested to Hall that she sell her house in St. Joseph and her farm upstate, and use the proceeds to buy the motel without having to resort to a kidnapping, but Hall vetoed that suggestion. He wanted much more money than those two sales would generate.

That Wednesday evening, Hall and Heady drove to the Coates House, a hotel on the corner of Broadway and 10th Street in Kansas City, to have dinner. A historic landmark that was once among the city's fanciest hotels, with a marble staircase leading off an ornate lobby, it was their favourite place to have dinner. Grover Cleveland had spent his honeymoon at the hotel. Hall and Heady always sat at the same table, when it was available, and enjoyed exchanging pleasantries with the same waitress.

After ordering, Hall excused himself, entered a phone booth, closed the door after him, and stuck a handkerchief in one side of his mouth in an effort to disguise his voice. Then he dialled GIlmore 6200, the number of the Greenlease home. It was now 8 P.M., fifty-eight hours after Bobby had been taken from school. Johnson, who by now had decided to help monitor calls, picked up the receiver.

Hall said, "This is M."

"What did you say?" Johnson asked.

"M," Hall repeated.

He then mentioned the Jerusalem medal, and gruffly informed Johnson to have the ransom ready by Thursday night. Rejoining Heady, he finished eating his meal. Afterwards, he and Heady returned to their home in St. Joseph.

The next day, Thursday, October 1, Heady cancelled the order for the new Studebaker, explaining that she had changed her mind. A bank official remembered that she was smartly dressed. She then rented a blue 1952 Ford sedan from the McCord-Bell U-Drive-It agency on 7th Street in St. Joseph. Hall drove it to North Kansas

City, with Heady following in her station wagon. He then abandoned the station wagon in the parking lot of a service station across from Lynn's Tavern, stole another set of licence plates from a car parked on a nearby street, put those on the rented Ford, and threw its plates away. Hall worried that passers-by and casual witnesses might have seen a woman driving the 1951 Plymouth station wagon who matched the description of the alleged aunt who took Bobby out of school. He was carrying his Smith & Wesson as he made his rounds, but he did not call the Greenlease family as he had promised.

After returning to St. Joseph, Hall and Heady had lunch at the Hoof and Horn Restaurant. In the evening, he scoured the personal ads in the *Star*, which was delivered daily to Heady's home, and saw the response to his classified advertisement that he had been waiting for. It read: "M: Meet me in Chicago Sunday. G."

The following Friday afternoon, Hall drove to Kansas City and placed another call to the Greenlease residence between 8:30 and 9:00 P.M. Again, he used a handkerchief to disguise his voice. Evincing no fear that his calls might be traced, Hall—in this and every other call to the family—seemed in no hurry to hang up as quickly as possible.

O'Neill answered, and Hall told him that he would be calling later that night with the instructions for the drop-off.

"Is Bobby all right?" O'Neill asked.

"He is fine but homesick," Hall answered.

In a sick joke, he claimed that he was even "earning" his ransom money because little Bobby was proving to be such a handful. He ended the conversation by saying, "Tonight," and hung up.

Hall then began to mark off the route that intermediaries for the Greenlease family were to follow when delivering the ransom. He had purchased medical adhesive tape at Herman's Drug Store in St. Joseph, and later some red chalk at a Katz Drug Store in North Kansas City. His first stop was at the intersection of 29th and Holmes streets in Kansas City, where he taped a note under a mailbox that told the intermediaries to proceed to 42nd and

Charlotte streets and look under the corner mailbox. At that intersection, he used the chalk to draw a cross on a rock, and placed a second set of instructions under it. This second note ordered the Greenlease family to deposit the ransom money in an outdoor alcove of the First Brethren Church at 40th and Harrison. Accompanying Hall, as he laid out the delivery route, was an inebriated and completely oblivious Heady. As Heady later confessed, she wanted to stay drunk because her conscience had begun to bother her, and she did not want to think about the horrible crime she had helped to perpetrate.

On October 2, Edward R. Murrow on *CBS TV News*, still only a fifteen-minute evening news programme with limited national distribution, and *The Kansas City Star* reported that the Greenlease family had received a demand for a $500,000 ransom. Ledterman, as family spokesman, immediately denied the claim. "No figure has been mentioned," he said. "We have not been in contact with the kidnapper." Murrow also reported that the family had been in contact with the kidnappers since shortly after the abduction, and that Greenlease was being subjected to a series of tests to prove his "good faith." The newspaper further noted that "an advertisement in the personals column of the *Star* this week was said to be part of the 'good faith' test."

"It was apparent that anxiety was mounting at the home," the *Star* reported. "Ledterman said he tried to ease his tension last night by walking. He made ten trips around the circular driveway at the home, and finally went to bed about 1 o'clock."

The Greenlease kidnapping was now a nationwide sensation. The abduction was not only front-page news in the Kansas City and St. Louis newspapers, but also on those of *The New York Times* and most other major newspapers. *Time* and other magazines also covered the kidnapping, and Murrow's near nightly broadcasts about the tragedy made it the first American crime to be covered evening after evening on national television. The crew of NBC's evening national news programme—the 15-minute *Camel News Caravan* with host John Cameron Swayze—reported on the kidnapping from its position outside the fence of the French Institute of Notre Dame de Sion. Not since the Lindbergh kidnapping in 1932, and, in the previous decade, Nathan Leopold and Richard Loeb's thrill-killing abduction and murder of Bobby Franks, had a crime so fascinated the entire nation.

The abduction had become international news as well, with reporters calling from England, Italy, and other countries. Both the public and the media, except for a very few reporters sworn to secrecy, remained unaware that the Greenleases had been in contact with the kidnappers, with both the local police department and FBI declining comment. *Newsweek* ran a news item titled "Where's Bobby?" in its National Affairs section. A photograph of Bobby and his father accompanied the story over a caption reading: "Bobby and dad: No news, bad news." In the absence of hard news to report, the *Star* noted that the fall foliage and a gentle rain had even "brought a scene of autumn tranquillity" to the Greenlease estate. Indoors, though, all was suspense and high drama, with Bobby Greenlease's life seemingly in the balance.

Many people assumed that organized crime was involved since so much money seemed to rule out anything an individual criminal was capable of planning. Kansas City, after all, had a well-deserved reputation as a haven for mobsters, and the era of Pretty Boy Floyd and Boss Pendergast still resonated in the city's collective consciousness.

To assist in the search for Bobby, the International Brotherhood of Teamsters announced that it was printing a circular with a photograph and a detailed description of the boy that would be posted at union halls throughout the country. In Washington, the head of the AFL National Association of Letter Carriers urged the union's 120,000 members to keep a lookout for Bobby. Reports of a woman and a boy in a car were now coming in from various parts of the country. In Wichita Falls, Texas, police even put up a roadblock after one such sighting. The Associated Press also reported that the Reverend Dr. Braxton Bragg Sawyer, a Baptist minister at Fort Smith, Arkansas, who broadcast daily into Arkansas, Missouri, and Kansas, offered to act as intermediary, but declared that under no circumstances would he deliver ransom money.

At 1:35 in the morning of Saturday, October 3, Hall again called the Greenlease home, this time from a bar located near the intersection of Troost and Armour streets in Kansas City, while Heady waited in the car. The bar was just about to close when Hall showed up. O'Neill answered and said, "Identify yourself." Hall replied, "This is M. Ribbon." This time he told O'Neill to go to 29th and Holmes streets, where he would find further instructions about delivering the ransom beneath a mailbox.

The police and FBI, while recording Hall's phone calls to the Greenlease home, were complying with the family's request that they be allowed to negotiate with the kidnappers directly. Law enforcement officials also agreed not to follow family emissaries when the ransom was delivered. The *Detroit Times* was to report months later that the FBI knew Hall was the kidnapper the day after Bobby disappeared. But the bureau did not know where he was, and feared arresting him because of the possibility that Hall belonged to a gang. Hall's first ransom note had been immediately flown to Washington, where his fingerprints were matched with those of his service records.*

---

*Hall's correspondence with the Greenlease family was undoubtedly forwarded to FBI headquarters in Washington, D.C., for forensic examination, as the *Detroit Times* noted. But nowhere in the FBI files on the Greenlease case is there any evidence that the agency knew that Carl Austin Hall was one of the kidnappers, or even that fingerprints of any kind had been successfully taken from the ransom demands. Nor did any other newspaper or news sources subsequently claim that the FBI knew the identity of the kidnapper soon after Bobby's abduction.

O'Neill and Johnson drove to the spot, and after considerable searching found a piece of paper rolled into one of the four legs of the box. Driving away from the scene, they quickly opened the note, only to discover that they had unearthed a grade school pupil's spelling test, with three words out of twenty-five misspelled and marked in red pencil by a teacher. Frantically rushing back to the mailbox, they resumed their search, and this time found the piece of paper taped to the underside. The note said: "Drive to the Greenlease used car lot at 29th and McGee. Leave your car. Exchange it for the second car in the middle row—a black one."

The two men did as directed, but since no one was on duty at the lot at that hour, no keys were available for the black car. Having no choice but to ignore that part of the note, they followed the next instruction, which directed them to another mailbox at 42nd and Charlotte streets. The printing was so childish that at first they wondered if Bobby had been made to write the note, though a handwriting expert later determined that he had not.

This time O'Neill and Johnson easily discovered the second note taped to the underside of the mailbox. It told them that the designated ransom delivery spot was the "first alcove of the First Brethren church" at 40th and Harrison. Two outdoor alcoves were built into the church's wall. (As with his first ransom note, Hall had again provided inaccurate instructions. The church's actual name was the Telescope Memorial Evangelical United Brethren Church.) This note instructed them: "Leave money here drive straight home boy fine if money ok he will be home in 24 hrs."

However, newspaper delivery boys had begun to assemble in the neighbourhood, and any passer-by would be able to see the delivery point from the street. The two men returned to the Greenlease home for a family conference. Robert Greenlease and his advisers decided that a note should be written to the kidnappers, informing them that the money was in the city and at the family's disposal, and using the excuse that it had not been available before dawn that day. O'Neill, who wrote the note, also asked the kidnappers to call with further instructions. He returned to the church with the note and placed it in the alcove, as Hall directed. A short time later, a passer-by saw the white envelope containing the note, realized that it concerned the Greenlease kidnapping, and immediately turned it over to the police.

When O'Neill and Ledterman returned to the Greenlease house, they noticed for the first time that Hall's original letter of instruction contained a further note on the envelope:

> Go to your used car lot take money and change to dark used car rember you are being watched—if contact man is picked up boy dies if everything is okay boy will be home in 24 hrs. Go next to adress on envelope—next message will be under mail box. M. Take zigzag route make sure you arnt followed you keep you bargain we will keep ours.

Meanwhile, Hall and Heady had driven around aimlessly in their rented Ford until about 4 A.M. They then headed towards the mailbox where they had left a further message, and discovered that it was still in place. Driving to a telephone booth located under a streetcar shelter at Brush Creek and Main streets, Hall again called the Greenlease residence to find out what had gone wrong. Ledterman nervously explained that the Greenlease family was confused by his instructions, and also that it did not have the money at home. He also expressed the fear that it would be daylight before the family could comply with the kidnappers' demand, and said that a message for the kidnappers had been left at the church. Satisfied by this explanation, Hall said, "I will call you later," and hung up. But he did not go to the church to pick up the message that they claimed to have left, fearing a trap.

Hall and Heady returned to their home in St. Joseph. That night, Heady called a man named Robert Castle, who lived in St. Joseph, and instructed him to pick up her boxer and take it to the Velflick

Kennels, explaining that she would be gone for several days. She wanted the dog to have proper care.

Hall and Heady remained in St. Joseph until early Saturday afternoon, October 3. They then drove to the Park-A-Nite Motel in North Kansas City at the intersection of U.S. Highways 71 and 69, taking an end cabin. They signed in as Mr. and Mrs. V. E. Heady, of Boonville, Missouri. At 12:14 A.M. on Sunday morning, they drove to the Town House Hotel in Kansas City, Kansas, and Hall again called the Greenlease residence. O'Neill answered and immediately handed the phone over to Virginia Greenlease, who always sat near the telephone during Hall's phone calls, and who by now was almost hysterical. The call lasted nearly nine minutes, the longest of any of the calls to the house, and Bobby's mother pleaded with the kidnapper for the safe return of her son—who by now had been dead a week. The police recorded this conversation:

VIRGINIA GREENLEASE: We have the money, but we must know our boy is alive and well. Can you give me that? Can you give me anything that will make me know that?

HALL: A reasonable request, but to be frank with you, the boy has been just about to drive us crazy. We couldn't risk taking him to a phone.

VG: Well, I can imagine that. Would you do this? Would you do this? Would you ask him two questions? Give me the answer to two questions . . .

HALL: Speaking.

VG: . . . and we could follow instructions and have everything ready if I had the answer to these two questions. I would know my boy is alive.

HALL: All right.

VG: Ask him what is the name of our driver in Europe this summer.

HALL: All right.

VG: Do you have that?

HALL: Yes.

VG: And the second question—what did you build with your monkey blocks . . .

HALL: All right.

VG:. . . in your playroom the last night you were home. Now, one reason I'm asking you this is because we have other people who claim they have Bobby, and if I can get the answers from you, I'll know you have him and he is alive, which is the thing you know that I want.

HALL: We have the boy. He is alive. Believe me. He's been driving us nuts.

VG: Well, I can imagine that. He's such an active youngster.

HALL: He's been driving us nuts.

VG: Could you get those answers?

HALL: All right.

At 1:35 that same Sunday morning, Hall phoned again, suggesting that he had talked to his confederates.

HALL: Lady, I called them and he wouldn't say anything. He just dummied up and he wouldn't say anything.

VG: We need to know that you have the boy and he is alive.

HALL: Lady, he is very much alive to date. He almost beat me over the head with a ball bat.

VG: I know he is a very active boy.

HALL: I know he comes from a good family. We have treated him well. We didn't beat the information out of him.

VG: Well, can you tell me how soon he will be released?

HALL: As soon as we have the money, he will be released in twenty-four hours in another town.

VG: We are anxious to see him. Can you tell me when he will be released?

HALL: In another city in twenty-four hours. Believe me, he's driving us crazy. I couldn't get the information. Did my best—

believe me. He talks about a parrot, Polly, and said he whistled.

VG: We are ready to make the payoff, if you can assure me my boy is all right.

HALL: The boy is well. I saw him this afternoon.

VG: We are ready to make the payoff . . .

HALL: We'll carry out our bargain if you carry yours out. I assure you your boy is safe—he is a hell-cat—lady, we have earned this money . . .

Hall then told O'Neill to go to "13 West Summit and you will find a note under a stone with a red crayon 'X' on it." Hall also directed O'Neill to stop using the two-tone blue-grey Oldsmobile he had been driving, and to begin driving Robert Greenlease's blue Cadillac. O'Neill and Ledterman drove to the intersection of 13th and Summit, only to discover that there was no such address as 13 West Summit. While searching the area for a note from the kidnapper, the two men were approached by a neighbour who had observed their movements and become suspicious. O'Neill explained that he was on a scavenger hunt, and that he was looking for "the last item and then I can go home." Satisfied, the man left. O'Neill and Ledterman decided a large stone on the southwest corner of the intersection was the one under which Hall had placed the note; but, try as they might, the two men simply could not get the stone to budge. Finally, they resumed looking elsewhere, and found the right stone with the following instructions:

Tie a white rag on your radio aerial. Proceed north on highway No. 169 (in Clay County) past the junction with highway No. 69 about three miles where you will come to Henry's place. Turn back one-half block and across the highway under a sign reading "Oakview, Inc." you will find another note.

That virtually incomprehensible second note—and one that yet again contained the wrong directions—read:

> Go back to Jt. (Viona Rd)—Go west to first rd heading south
> across from lum reek farm sign. Drive in 75 ft. leave bag on right
> side of road. Drive home, will call and tell you where you can
> pickup boy.

Translation: Return to the junction. Turn west on Vivion Road, also known as U.S. Highway 69. Continue to a road—Old Pike Road—across from a sign for the Lum Reek farm. Proceed for seventy-five feet. Leave the money on the right side of the road.

O'Neill twice missed the turn-off. It was raining hard that night, and in the dark he and Ledterman became confused by the series of farm lanes about where exactly the drop site was. The two men also had no idea what a "lum reek farm sign" referred to. Continuing to head west, they finally found a car parked outside a roadside tavern. Sitting inside were a young boy and girl. O'Neill asked them where Lum Reek was located and the young man told O'Neill to follow him. When they reached the road, he said, he would flash his lights. When they reached the spot, the man flashed his lights and drove on, and O'Neill swung down Old Pike Road—a dirt lane—for seventy-five feet. Then he and Ledterman deposited the duffel bag, weighing eighty-five pounds and containing the $600,000 in ransom, at what they hoped was the specified drop-off site.

Hall, with Heady asleep beside him, had driven to Highway 69 near that point and saw the dark Cadillac sedan go by, and assumed it was the payoff car. After driving down the dirt road, he looked for the duffel bag, but could not find it. He then drove back to Kansas City, Kansas, and placed another call from a phone booth in the Town House Hotel to the Greenlease residence, and was informed that the ransom had been dropped off and that he should go back and look for it. Hall did drive back to look for it, but again could not find it. Calling the Greenlease residence a third time, at 4:32 A.M., he was told that the Greenlease intermediaries were on their way to pick up the money for fear that some unauthorized person might find it. Hall, who sounded drunk, apologized, saying the mix-up had been his mistake, and promised to call again later in the day. He was determined that the drop-off be made on that Sunday, and he again said that Bobby would be delivered twenty-four hours after the ransom was paid. Two hours after they had dropped the money off, O'Neill and Ledterman rushed back to pick it up again. The duffel bag had not been disturbed.

Hall had made four calls that morning, sounding drunk each time. Most of the Greenlease family's advisers had concluded by now that Bobby was probably dead. Hall had failed to provide any of the answers Mrs. Greenlease had requested. (On his last night at home, Bobby had built an Eiffel Tower with blocks.) Yet they were eager to cooperate with Hall anyway in the slim hope that the boy was alive.

On Sunday afternoon, Hall and Heady checked into Tiny and Maria's Hotel on East Highway 40, taking the end cabin. A very drunk Heady passed out and remained in bed for the rest of the day. Hall spent the afternoon laying out the route for the third payoff attempt, finally deciding on County Road 10E, which ran south off Highway 40 to a bridge a mile away that spanned the Little Blue River. The bridge, he decided, would be where the money was to be finally handed over. After he returned to the motel, he and Heady checked out, some time around 8 P.M.

Hall had told the Greenlease family that he would call them at eight that evening, but he did not call until 8:30, apologizing for his tardiness. He placed the call from a Katz Drug Store at Lynnwood and Troost streets in Kansas City, and talked to Ledterman.

"Let's get this thing over," Ledterman said.

Hall assured Ledterman that he would send a telegram in care of Western Union that would tell him where to pick up Bobby.

"You're not bunking me on that, are you?" Ledterman asked.

"That's the gospel truth," Hall replied.

Clearly annoyed by all the mix-ups and inaccurate directions

Hall had given the family, an exasperated Ledterman could barely contain his fury when he continued: "This idea of climbing the tree and looking in a bird's nest for a note, then climbing on your belly somewhere looking for something under a rock with a red, white, and blue ribbon around it—that's getting tiresome. You know, you and I don't have to play ball that way. We can deal man to man."

"There will be no mix-up tonight," Hall promised. "It will go perfectly."

So far, Hall had sent the Greenlease family more than a half-dozen letters and made fifteen telephone calls. Now, though, despite his assurances, he was about to give the family their most complicated instructions yet. First, he told Ledterman that, after the ransom drop, he should drive to Pittsburg, Kansas, a town one hundred miles south of Kansas City near the Oklahoma border. After registering under his own name at a hotel there, he was to contact Western Union. A telegram would arrive telling him where to pick up Bobby.

He then said that the family should expect another call that night, at exactly 11:30, at a Kansas City hotel telephone booth with the phone number VAlentine 9279. At that time, said Hall, he would provide further instructions on when and where to make the drop. When Ledterman prodded him on the name of the hotel, Hall, who was slurring his words, admitted that he could not remember the hotel's name.

"Suppose I call VAlentine 9279 and I don't get an answer?" Ledterman said. "How am I going to find out what the hotel is?"

Hall said that the hotel might be near Linwood and Troost streets in downtown Kansas City, near the Lasalle Hotel, though he could not be sure. Apologetically, he also said that the hotel's name might end in "shire." The police quickly determined that the telephone booth was in the Berkshire Hotel.

That evening, O'Neill sat in a car guarding the $600,000 while Ledterman went into the Berkshire Hotel. At exactly 11:31 Hall called, identifying himself as usual as M, and told Ledterman to head east on U.S. Highway 40 until he reached county Highway 10E, also known as Lee's Summit Road. Ledterman was to turn south "alongside Stephenson's restaurant" and continue for about one mile until he came to a wooden bridge. He was to throw the bag out on the right side of the road on the north side of the bridge. Hall indicated that he would be following from a short distance.

Hall, parked near a filling station from where he made the phone call, eventually saw the dark Cadillac going east on Highway 40 that he assumed contained Ledterman and an associate. Heady was with Hall in the rented Ford as he waited, but she was too drunk to understand what was happening.

This time, Ledterman and O'Neill succeeded in making the drop exactly where Hall had specified—an isolated crossroads on a county road east of Kansas City. The time was around midnight. Dressed as always in suits, with white shirts and ties and brown fedoras, the two men lugged the eighty-five-pound bag from the car and placed it under some underbrush beneath the wooden bridge.

Three or four minutes after Ledterman passed by, Hall drove down 10E toward Highway 40, but did not see the bag, and continued heading south for several miles. He then turned around and headed north, turned off the engine and headlights, and waited. About ten minutes later, he turned on the ignition again and drove past the Cadillac, which was now coming toward him. As soon as he crossed over the wooden bridge, he stopped on the north side, got out, retrieved the duffel bag, and put it in the trunk. The time was now about 12:30 A.M., Monday, October 5.

To calm his nerves, Hall had taken a quarter-gram of morphine before the ransom pick-up, and he and Heady had also stopped frequently at various bars, before and after the drop, for a shot or two of whisky. In addition, they also drank from a bottle of whisky they kept in the car.

After they picked up the money, Heady wanted to return to St. Joseph. But Hall decided to keep on going down the highway, though he had no particular destination in mind. Suddenly panicking, he feared that when he had passed the Cadillac containing Ledterman, the Greenlease emissary had been able to take down the licence plate of the rented Ford.

"Well, we go back there," he told Heady, "they are going to be sitting in the front yard waiting for us, because it's a chance, because I don't know that they didn't get that number. Maybe they didn't. There's only one thing to do, and that's to get to St. Louis, and we will try to get straightened out there and make our plans from there."

They continued to argue, and finally Heady agreed to his spur-of-the-moment plan to hide out in St. Louis. But she insisted that, when they did get there, "Let's go to the Chase," referring to the city's premier hotel. Hall, who was unfamiliar with the city and had only passed through it once on his way to Chicago, explained, "If I am hot, that will be the first place they will look, because they will turn every policeman out in the United States in this thing. That's the first place they do is check the cabs and see if they went to a hotel." Later, he said, "I'll get a car and drive to an apartment, rent an apartment where there won't be any cab records of going to an apartment and renting it."

Hall had between $80 and $100 of his own money in his wallet. A half-hour after the pick-up, he stopped at a bar on the corner of 31st and Forest streets in Kansas City that he knew would still be open, to make one last cruel call to the Greenlease residence.

"We got the bag," he informed Ledterman. He also jokingly remarked, "We made more tonight than we did all last week," adding, "I might buy a Cadillac." Once again, he assured Ledterman that he would send a wire in the morning to Western Union in Pittsburg, Kansas, telling him where to pick up Bobby, and promising him that the boy was alive and well, and "full of hell." "You can tell his mother," he said, "that she will see him as we promised within twenty-four hours."

Ledterman asked, "The boy is alive and well?"

Hall replied, "And as full of piss as any kid I've ever seen."

"I can quote you on that, can I?"

"Yes, you can quote me."

Ledterman and O'Neill left for Pittsburg sometime around three o'clock, arriving around 5:30 A.M. At the hotel, they asked the management to wake them at seven o'clock, when the Western Union office opened. After a brief rest, the two men went to the telegraph office as soon as it opened, informed the management that they were expecting an urgent message and needed it delivered to them as soon as possible.

Still hoping against hope that Bobby would soon safely be returned to them, the two men had brought along a clean suit, new underwear, some socks, and a topcoat to keep Bobby warm on the return trip.

After a fruitless two-day wait, the two men returned home.

By the time Hall and Heady embarked on the 243 mile drive across Missouri, both were drunk. Since they had not thought to have a backup plan, neither had brought luggage, toiletries, or anything else that might prove useful on a trip. But Hall did have enough wits about him to pull the car over, soon after leaving the city, to change the licence plates. Using a flashlight, he also opened the trunk and raised the flap of the duffel bag to make sure that it actually contained the ransom. Reassured, he wrestled out one package of bills consisting of about $6,000, returned to the car, and remarked to Heady that he had never seen so much money.

3.

The Shady Motel

The highway was mostly empty as Hall and Heady continued to fly eastward. The official speed limit was seventy miles per hour, so that even at eighty or slightly more, at that time of night, they would have attracted little notice.

They made several other stops, besides the ones to call the Greenleases and to switch licence plates, as they proceeded to St. Louis. Hall suffered from a kidney condition requiring him to pull over frequently on the highway shoulder to urinate. He also stopped somewhere to buy a carton of cigarettes.

The route across the middle of the state eventually brought them to Boonville, home of the Kemper Military School, where Hall and Paul Greenlease had been cadets twenty years earlier. Here he apparently stopped at an all-night café to refill the gas tank and get matches.

During the rest of the drive, Hall and Heady, by his estimate, spoke no more than ten words. For much of the time, she either slept or had passed out. When she awoke, it was to smoke a cigarette and take another drink of whisky before falling back to sleep.

They finally arrived in St. Louis around six in the morning on Monday, October 5. Finding the Sportsman's Bar & Grill at 3500 South Jefferson Avenue open, Hall parked the car near the corner of Potomac Street, leaving the money locked in the trunk. After ordering drinks for each of them, he used the tavern's phone to call attorney Barney Patton at his home in St. Joseph.

Patton was literally the only person in the world whom Hall felt he could trust. The attorney had been instrumental in helping him obtain his parole, and had done him several other favours, including finding him a job as an automobile salesman when he got out of prison. A grateful Hall had later invited Patton to Heady's home for dinner. Patton reciprocated by inviting Hall and Heady to dinner at the home of his parents, in one of the city's best residential neighbourhoods.

Panicky and paranoid, and all but certain that Ledterman and O'Neill had been able to take down his licence plate number, Hall asked the lawyer to contact the McCord-Bell car rental agency and somehow arrange to alter or destroy the record showing that the Ford had been rented in Heady's name. Patton declined and asked why Hall wanted him to do that. Hall refused to say why, explaining only that he had been in some trouble in Kansas City, and the two men left the matter at that. Hall and Heady sat drinking in the Sportsman's Bar for some time. They also entered a nearby diner and ordered breakfast, but neither was able to eat much and they soon left.

Hall's next order of business, now that the police would certainly be looking for the kidnappers and the ransom money, was to abandon the Ford rental. He called the Yellow Cab Company, asking for a car to pick him up. It arrived about fifteen minutes later. Both Hall and Heady got in, and Hall directed the driver, George Oberbeck, to find a luggage store. After scouting the downtown area, the three of them found the Broadway Army Store at 17 North Broadway, which Hall thought would be opening its doors at 9 A.M.—still some minutes away. To pass the time, he invited the driver to join him and Heady at Slay's Bar at 114 North Broadway, where Hall had one and Heady two shots of Walkers Deluxe straight whisky, while Oberbeck ordered a Coca-Cola.

At some point, Hall left Heady and Oberbeck, went into the luggage store, and purchased a green metal footlocker and a smaller black metal suitcase. He set both pieces of luggage on the sidewalk next to the cab, and summoned Heady and Oberbeck, who put the footlocker and suitcase into the trunk. Oberbeck drove them back to the Sportsman's Bar and Hall paid him. After putting the luggage in the Ford, he and Heady drove to a quiet, brick-paved alley lined with ash pits and a few garages behind nearby Wyoming Street. When he opened the trunk, he had to use a penknife to cut the drawstrings around the top of the duffel bag because it was tied so tightly. Laying the footlocker and suitcase on the alley, he then quickly dumped the money into both pieces of luggage. The ransom filled both of them to the very top, forcing him to dispose of a metal tray in one so that all of the bills could fit in snugly. Fearful of being observed, they did not bother to count the money. When a couple drove past them in the alley, Hall moved one of the suitcases to allow the other car to get by, and afterwards waved to the driver, saying, "It's okay."

By now it was about 9:30 A.M. Disposing of the duffel bag in a trash can, Hall and Heady next drove to the nearby Hi-Nabor Buffet at 2801 Wyoming Street, where they brought both the footlocker and metal suitcase into the tavern and had a few more drinks. They remained there for about forty-five minutes. Hall briefly left Heady alone at the bar while he drove the Ford to the 2800 block of nearby Utah Street and abandoned it. Returning to the bar, he again called for a Yellow Cab. When it arrived, Hall transferred the footlocker and suitcase once more, and told Irwin Rosa, the driver, to take him to a "used car row." Almost immediately, a drunken Heady demanded instead to be taken to the bus station downtown. Perhaps to avoid a loud and possibly incriminating confrontation in the presence of a potential witness, Hall uncharacteristically agreed. At the Greyhound Bus Depot at Broadway and Delmar Avenue downtown, Rosa helped Hall set the two pieces of luggage on the sidewalk. Hall paid the $1.25 fare with two one-dollar bills. By now it was about 10:35 A.M.

While in the bus station, Hall and Heady argued about whether to go to a hotel or try to rent an apartment. An agitated Heady went up to the ticket agent, Glenn C. Hartley, and asked about bus service to Kansas City; Tripp, South Dakota; and Bismarck, North Dakota. She also asked him about travellers insurance. Hall, not to be dissuaded, consulted the Yellow Pages, looking for the address of a used car lot. Selecting one on South Kingshighway, a major north–south boulevard, he hailed another cab that dropped them off at Columbo's Bar at 3132 South Kingshighway, their fourth bar stop that morning. Again they brought the footlocker and metal suitcase in with them.

After ordering more drinks for themselves, Hall made another call to Patton from a phone booth in the bar to find out whether he had destroyed the rental car record.

"When did you rent this car?" a suspicious Patton asked. The lawyer had begun to wonder whether the Ford had been used in the Greenlease kidnapping.

"Thursday or Friday, October 1 or 2," Hall replied.

That answer allayed Patton's fears. He then asked if Heady was in some kind of trouble.

"It doesn't concern you or me," Hall told him.

"You aren't running away from a hit-and-run case, are you?" Patton persisted. "If you are, I don't want to get mixed up in it."

Hall assured Patton that Heady was not involved in any such case. He offered to send any amount of money Patton required to do the favour, if he would only not ask any questions. Patton again refused. Nevertheless, Hall informed the lawyer that the car would be left in the 2800 block of Wyoming Street. In fact, though, he had gotten yet another address wrong.

After downing a few more drinks, Hall and Heady began

arguing about where to go next. She insisted on booking a room at the Chase Hotel in the Central West End, but Hall had enough of his wits about him to realize that walking into a hotel lobby in the company of a very inebriated woman would attract attention.

Soon after 11 A.M., Hall walked to the Barrett-Weber Ford used car lot across the street and bought a 1947 maroon four-door Nash sedan. Lindsay Worley, the salesman, at first told him the price was $350; but after spotting an easy mark and consulting the manager, he upped the price to $425. Hall agreed to the sale, paid for the car with the ransom money, returned to the bar, and waited for Worley to bring the necessary papers for him to sign. He identified himself as Steve Strand on the sales contract.

When a drunken Heady saw the Nash, she fell into a rage. "What on earth?" she cried out. "Where did you get that?" She had wanted Hall to buy a new car and not one that was six years old.

Hall tried to explain that an old car would not draw attention to them, but she refused to be placated.

Hall had also bought a morning newspaper, and the bartender helped him look through the classifieds in search of a furnished apartment to rent nearby. They soon found one on Arsenal Street, just around the corner from Kingshighway, and Hall dialled the number listed in the advertisement. When a woman answered, he learned that the apartment was still available and told her he would be right over to check it out. The bartender gave him directions.

Hall and Heady then drove to the apartment, at 4504 Arsenal Street. It faced upon Tower Grove Park, originally part of the country estate of Henry Shaw, an Englishman who had amassed a fortune after immigrating to St. Louis in the early 1800s. After Shaw's death, the land was donated to the city, and named Tower Grove because a grove of sassafras trees stood nearby. Despite facing such manicured grounds, sprinkled with gazebos and statuary, the residences lining Arsenal Street were modest, and many apartments were rented out by the week or month.

Coincidentally, the man who would mastermind Hall's imminent downfall lived just minutes away on the opposite side of the park.

When Hall and Heady arrived at the apartment, sometime around noon, Heady was so intoxicated that she could barely stand. The landlady introduced herself as Mary Webb, and Hall registered as John Grant of Elgin, Illinois, a town he had never been to. Identifying Heady as his wife Esther, he apologetically explained that she was quite ill, and said the two of them planned on remaining in St. Louis for about two months on an extended vacation. After paying Webb $20 for a week's rent in advance, and another $5 deposit for the key, he carried each suitcase separately into the apartment. They were too heavy for him to transport both at the same time. The footlocker weighed an estimated forty to fifty pounds, and the smaller one between thirty and thirty-five pounds. He also asked Webb where the nearest shopping area was. She told him that the closest was on nearby Morganford Road, but that he would find a better one on Grand and Arsenal, only a few blocks further on.

When Hall plopped Heady onto the bed, she immediately began to complain that the apartment was a "dump" and that she did not want to stay there. Hall agreed, saying, "I don't either. I don't blame you, but it's the only thing to do for the time being." But Heady kept repeating, "Let's go to the Chase Hotel." Hall punched her on the jaw and Heady passed out, ending the discussion. He then lay down himself for a few minutes, wondering frantically what to do with the money, and knowing that he could not trust Heady in her condition. Not for a moment did he fear that she might double-cross him, but he did worry that she was so erratic and unstable that she could betray him just by being herself. As his signed confession would later dryly note, Hall even fretted that Heady "might see a man out on the street she liked, invite him in, and give him a thousand dollars."

While Heady slept, Hall left the apartment. Though he had not brought along a change of clothes, he still looked dressed for success—snap-brim brown hat, tan sport shirt, and tweed brown coat. He drove the Nash to the Old Shillelagh Bar a few blocks away at 3157 Morganford Road. While enjoying a few more drinks, he wrote a letter to Patton. Curiously, now that he had money, the first thing Hall wanted to do was to show his gratitude for all the favours the St. Joseph attorney had done for him by sending him some cash. When Hall finished writing the letter, he wrapped it around $500 in $20 bills. After obtaining an envelope from the bartender, he addressed it to Patton, inserted the cash, and carefully sealed it. Noticing a cabdriver at the bar who was watching the sixth and deciding game of the World Series, he then decided to watch a few innings himself. Casey Stengel's Bronx Bombers, led by Billy Martin and Mickey Mantle, ultimately defeated the Brooklyn Dodgers in that 4–3 game.

After posting the letter to Patton in a nearby mailbox, Hall asked the cabdriver, Edward Gorman, if he would drive him to a shopping area where he might find an appliance store. Gorman agreed, but the expedition to nearby Hampton Village was unsuccessful. No appliance store was to be found. They returned to the bar, only to discover the Petruso Electrical Appliance Store nearby. Hall and Gorman both went in, and Hall purchased a CBS radio for $28 that he could use to listen to news broadcasts. He also asked for a cardboard box. When the clerk replied that he only had a larger-size box, Hall took the larger box—one measuring about fifteen by nineteen inches.

"It swims in this one," he remarked, pleased.

Gorman took him to a corner near the Arsenal Street apartment, and Hall walked the rest of the way. When he entered the apartment, he discovered that Heady was still asleep. He tried unsuccessfully to awaken her, plugged in the radio, and lay down. Too restless to remain in bed for more than a few minutes, he got up again and walked to the Squeeze Box Tavern at 3225

Morganford Road. Ordering a shot of whisky, he nervously paced the floor.

All morning, Hall had been desperately trying to form a plan, and at last something very like one began to take shape. Lost in a no-man's-land of his mind somewhere between extreme paranoia and utter recklessness, if not plain stupidity, Hall came up with the idea of dispatching a call girl to Los Angeles to mail yet another letter to Patton. Hall was convinced that the authorities would somehow intercept the letter, and confine their investigation to the West Coast. A man who in better times had spent plenty of money on call girls, he naively assumed that a prostitute would probably be pleased to earn the money without asking any questions. He apparently did not consider the possibility that an unscrupulous, street-savvy prostitute, sensing an opportunity to earn even more money, just might ask a question or two.

Not wanting to delay putting his plan into action, Hall asked the bartender for the Squeeze Box Tavern's address, and had him repeat it several times because he was having difficulty understanding the word "Morganford." Calling for a Laclede Cab, he left, having stayed at the tavern only fifteen minutes. Some moments later, Henry Schmidt, the bar's owner, went into the restroom, discovered a bank currency wrapper bearing the notation "$2,000," and flushed it down the toilet.

Hall told Howard A. Lewis, the Laclede driver who answered his call, to procure a girl for him. Lewis replied that "that stuff is not my business." But he did offer to try to locate a cabdriver who could be of more help. They drove downtown, but Lewis failed to find another driver willing to procure a woman for his customer. Hall then directed Lewis to return to his apartment at 4504 Arsenal, saying he wished to pick up some sample cases that he used in his job as a salesman. On the way, they stopped at Brownie's Tavern just east of Gravois Avenue on Arsenal, where Hall had a quick drink. They then proceeded to the apartment, and Hall asked Lewis to wait for him.

Heady was still asleep when Hall walked in. Moving quickly, he scrawled a quick note: "Had to move bags in a hurry as report came in on radio—Girl next door looked funny—Couldn't wake you—Stay here and I'll call when I can."

Hastily, he also wrote a second note: "Stay where you are baby. I will see you in short order. Tell them you are not well and they will bring you food. Just say your husband was called away unexpectedly."

He left behind $2,500, tucked into the bottom of Heady's purse. Carrying the footlocker and the metal suitcase one at a time, he took them to the front door, and Lewis helped put the former into the car's trunk. Since there was not enough room for the smaller case to fit, Hall kept it next to him on the back seat.

Hall instructed Lewis to continue to look for a woman, saying, "I want a nice girl," and making it clear that he did not want to be taken to a brothel. He also handed Lewis a $20 bill as "a token of good luck." As the cab headed downtown, he dozed briefly. Around 3:30, Lewis pulled up next to a cabbie parked in front of the Jefferson Hotel and asked if he could get his fare a girl. That driver, John Oliver Hager, who worked for Ace Cab, had a fare heading for Union Station, but said he could be of help. The two drivers agreed to meet shortly at the bar of the nearby Reed Hotel at 15th and Pine streets. When the two cabs met up, Hall paid his driver another $20, the footlocker and the metal suitcase were transferred from one cab to another, and Hager and Hall drove off. Hall identified himself as Steve Strand, and Hager told him he knew someone who might agree to be his date.

Ace Cab was to be Hall's doom. Joseph Costello, a local mobster, owned the company, but Hager never suspected that his fare might be the kidnapper whose shocking crime riveted the nation. He quickly saw that Hall had been drinking; guessed that his fare was, in his own words, "a good-time Charley"; and assumed that Hall's explanation that he needed a girl to carry a letter for him to Los Angeles was just a pretext, and that what Hall really wanted was a hooker. Hager, who lived in a cramped SRO room at the Lincoln Hotel near downtown, also worked as a part-time pimp for a prostitute named Sandra O'Day. An ex-convict, he had been sentenced to two years in the Missouri State Penitentiary in 1950 for passing bad cheques. In a remarkable near-coincidence, the two men were alumni of the same prison in Jefferson City; their periods of incarceration had missed overlapping only by a matter of months.

As they drove off, Hager asked Hall if he planned to spend the night with the woman, and where he wanted to go. Hall replied that he had no idea where to go, but that he might want to spend two or three nights with the prostitute.

In February 1940, J. Edgar Hoover, the director of the Federal Bureau of Investigation, had warned of a new threat to the American way of life. As the United States edged ever closer toward declaring war against Nazi Germany in Europe, Hoover published an article in *American Magazine* entitled "Camps of Crime" that singled out a relatively new enemy within—the roadside motel. Those anonymous establishments sprouting up on the country's wide-open roads were, according to Hoover, "a new home of crime in America, a new home of disease, bribery, corruption, crookedness, rape, white slavery, thievery, and murder."

He had a point.

Motels were an outgrowth of the country's enthusiasm for auto camps, whose popularity peaked in the years immediately following World War I. The mass production of automobiles provided thousands, and ultimately millions, of Americans with an unprecedented opportunity to travel for long distances within a relatively short time whenever and to wherever it suited them.

Privately owned auto camps with individual showers and bathrooms eventually evolved into tourist cabins or cottages—

usually mom-and-pop operations built around a simple theme. Log cabins and wigwams were among the popular motifs of the era. The popularity of motor courts soared when the federal government began construction of Route 66, the first concrete-paved, year-round highway linking the East and West Coasts. The last section of the highway was finally completed, in Arizona, in 1937. Not surprisingly, Route 66 eventually became affectionately known as the "Mother Road"—the primary if somewhat meandering national thoroughfare not only for tourists and travelling businessmen, but also for Army personnel and equipment being transferred to and from military bases.

That was the business climate in 1940 when Hoover called for an investigation of motels—the word concocted in 1925 by Californian Arthur Heineman, who created it by combining "motor court" and "hotel"—which had already acquired a reputation for seediness and immorality. A man who probably agreed with the FBI director's assessment of the dark purposes fuelling the popularity of motels was a St. Louis entrepreneur named John Carr. But whereas Hoover saw motels as potential cesspools of crime and immorality, Carr saw opportunity.

In 1942, two years after Hoover's article appeared in *American Magazine*, Carr opened a motel just outside the city limits of St. Louis that was destined to play a major role in the Greenlease case, and ultimately to become notorious in subsequent decades chiefly for its noir association with this horrific crime.

Carr had been the successful operator of a brothel in St. Louis, and later married the woman who had served as the establishment's madam. His home in the 3700 block of Washington Boulevard was well known as a rendezvous for professional bondsmen, some policemen, and what the *St. Louis Post-Dispatch* described as "police characters." Wanting to expand his business, he purchased 8.73 acres of land in the municipality of Marlborough, in south St. Louis County. St. Louis was a logical stopover point for travellers from points east of Chicago, and Carr's motel would give them an ideal place to resume their westward journey after an overnight stay. Marlborough was composed almost entirely of tourist courts and roadside establishments. Carr—who had a long police record—served as its treasurer, and the municipality's police department was notoriously corrupt.

But Carr also intended to exploit the reputation of motels for amoral assignations—exactly what Hoover was worried about— by creating a motel masterpiece, a roadside Shangri-la that would have no peer on Route 66. Hall and Heady may have harboured a similar vision when they talked of using some of the ransom money to operate their own motel in La Jolla.

Carr chose Adolph L. Struebig, a local architect, to design the motel. The original court, built in the Streamline Moderne style, a variant of Art Deco, consisted of ten single-storey, two-unit buildings, with a large manager's building closer to Route 66, which was also known locally as Watson Road. The flat-roofed, rounded-corner cabins, ultra-sleek for their time, were separated by garages that allowed visitors to seclude themselves with no telltale automobiles parked outside to announce their presence. Most of the windows consisted of glass blocks, further ensuring privacy. Each room also had its own private bathroom—the Moderne architectural motif referred to the fact that all rooms contained a private toilet, still an unusual feature at the time—and beds were equipped with Beautyrest mattresses. Carr christened the motel the Coral Court because the ceramic used as a veneer on the concrete walls was the colour of golden honey, or coral, with dark brown accents. A few years after World War II, he built twenty-three new buildings totalling forty-six rooms, with the final tally reaching seventy-seven.

Business was good from the start, with rooms available both for overnight accommodations and for four-hour rest periods. Highway rest areas were still more than a decade off, but the discount rate available to those who needed a room for only four hours quickly made the Coral Court locally infamous. Rumours that Carr had formerly operated a brothel in the city's midtown area, that he now ran a prostitution ring out of the motel, that he had mob connections, and that the employees had a reputation for being tight-lipped, only added to the Coral Court's no-questions-asked appeal. Such was its reputation on the evening of Monday, October 5, when Hager chose it as the logical place to deposit his most recent customer and call girl Sandra O'Day.

A rather plump, big-boned woman of medium height with long blond hair, twenty-two-year-old Sandra O'Day and her seven-year-old daughter lived with her aunt, Polly Lane, on St. Louis's North Side. Hager and O'Day, known as Sandy, had known each other for only a few months when Hall entered their lives. After they picked up O'Day at her house at 2023 North 9th Street, the three of them stopped at a tavern called McNamee's Bar at 2500 St. Louis Avenue for a couple of rounds each and to get acquainted. It was now mid-afternoon, around four. Hall excused himself to use the men's room. Hager, noticing a bulge in his coat, wondered if his fare was a policeman carrying a gun who was preparing to set a trap, and not a good-time Charley.

When he returned, Hall asked the bartender for a pencil, a piece of paper, and an envelope. He went to another table, wrote a note, put it into the envelope, sealed it, and addressed it to Esther Grant, Heady's pseudonym. After tucking the envelope into a pocket, he rejoined Hager and O'Day.

"Steve, I'm doing this for you only as a favour," Hager said. "But are you a cop?"

Hall laughed and said, "John, if you knew the truth, you'd really get a kick out of it."

Hall paid for the drinks with a $20 bill, and then shoved the $18 worth of change across the table to Hager, saying, "You take this."

"What a fare I've got here," Hager thought to himself, as they left the tavern.

Hall asked Hager to buy him some shaving gear, and Hager obliged by pulling up at the Sturgis Drug Store at 1701 South Grand Avenue. When Hall saw a Laclede Cab parked nearby, he told Hager to give the driver the note he had just written to Heady, and tell him to deliver it to Esther Grant at the address on the envelope—4504 Arsenal Street. Hager complied.

After buying shaving materials for Hall, Hager found a motorcycle policeman stopped beside his cab, which had been parked illegally. The policeman pointed to a NO PARKING sign and told the cabbie, "You guys are always squawking about not being able to park around town." As Hall squirmed in the back seat, the policeman lectured Hager on parking rules. When he finished, Hager drove to the Coral Court motel on Route 66, just outside the city limits, stopping along the way to pick up a fifth of David Nicholson 1843 Bonded Whiskey and four packs of Pall Mall cigarettes at the coincidentally named Hall Package Liquor at 5217 Chippewa Street. Once on their way again, Hall gave Hager five $20 bills and said, "Here, some money on account."

"Gee, what's this?" a by now thoroughly puzzled Hager thought. "I'm going to stick with this guy."

En route, O'Day asked Hall what was in his luggage. He replied that he was a pharmaceutical salesman, and that the luggage contained serum samples, adding curiously, "Animal or human, what's the difference?"

The cab reached the Coral Court between 4:30 and 5:00 P.M., and Hager checked to see if there were any vacancies. He soon returned, and told Hall that a room was available. Hall registered, giving his and O'Day's names as Mr. and Mrs. Robert White of Chicago. Pleased to learn that the rate was only $5.50 per day, he paid for three days in advance. During his trips to California, motel rates had been triple that amount in some places. Hager lugged both suitcases up to cabin 49-A, located on the top floor of a two-storey building.

Once inside, Hall hung his coat in a closet, and he and Hager had a drink or two from the whisky bottle. Feeling comfortable with his two companions, Hall began to relax somewhat, and told them, "Money doesn't mean anything. I trust you two kids. Sometimes I go on a bender for three or four days. I like to have a good time and maybe spend two or three thousand dollars."

Going over to his coat, he took a fistful of $20s from a pocket and sat down on the bed, trying to count the money. Hager's eyes bulged. When O'Day interrupted Hall, he lost count, much to his annoyance. He then handed the money to the cabdriver and asked him to count it, explaining that he was half-drunk. Hager reported that the sum came to $2,480. Hall gave Hager another $20, to make it an even $2,500, saying, "John, I want you to keep this for me."

Realizing that his shirt was dirty and that he had no other clothing, Hall asked Hager to buy him a white silk shirt, some underwear, and socks, and to bring them to his room around ten that night. Then, he suggested, the three of them could go nightclubbing. Knowing that she was not suitably dressed for such an evening out, O'Day asked Hager to get a dress and other apparel from her aunt Polly.

Hall opened the closet, retrieved his .38 calibre revolver, and showed it to his two guests, remarking, "Ain't this a beaut?"

O'Day agreed that the gun looked "cute," but took it from him and removed the shells. A gun, she sarcastically explained, was just what she needed. Then she handed it back. Her remarks angered Hall, who told her that he had more cartridges in his pocket; but when he pulled out a handful to display as proof, Hager and O'Day both thought they were .25 calibre, too small for Hall's revolver. Most likely, they were for Heady's gun. Hall explained that he kept the pistol for protection because he often carried around a considerable sum of money.

Hager was dispatched to buy some beer, and soon returned with three bottles of Budweiser and two cigars that he purchased at a nearby bar, Connor's Pink House. Knowing that Hall and O'Day planned on going out that evening, and that his own services might be needed, Hager asked the manager for a business card to give to Hall. The cabbie thought he could simply wait at the bar until his fare—Steve Strand—called him.

Hager later went out to buy sandwiches for all of them. While the cabdriver was gone, Hall gave O'Day $200. The money was still lying on the bed when Hager returned with some egg sandwiches, and O'Day handed him the money, asking that he give it to her aunt Polly. Hager's arrangement with O'Day was that he took a 40 percent cut of her earnings. Around six o'clock, he left.

O'Day wanted to go to bed immediately, but Hall, who had not slept for at least forty-eight hours, and not eaten in three or four days, knew that he could not perform sexually. Nor did he particularly want to, since he had hired O'Day for another purpose. "I paid your money," he told her. "I've got something I want you to do, so relax." But O'Day grew restless and annoyed at this rebuff, and continued to grouse while watching television. Hall went on drinking until finally, giving in to her complaints, he said, "Well, go on in and get cleaned up." Moments later, he confessed, "I haven't been to bed for five days. The last thing I want is sex."

Then he explained, "I got you here for one reason, and I will tell you what that is later."

O'Day, though, went in to take a bath, later reemerged, and continued to complain, saying, "What kind of deal is this?"

She sensed that she had found an easy, generous mark, and wanted to capitalize on her opportunity in the only way she knew—through sex.

"Don't worry," Hall said, trying to soothe her once more, "you got your money."

Trying another tack, O'Day mentioned that she had a daughter. Also, she told Hall, she owned a farm, and asked him for money to buy a bull because she wanted to raise prize show cattle.

"Why would anyone want to spend money for a bull?" Hall thought. "Whisky, yes, but not a bull."

"Is that all you want money for?" he asked.

"I want to buy a big Guernsey bull," she said. "If you would buy me a bull, I would be the happiest woman on earth."

If O'Day would fly to Los Angeles and mail a letter for him, Hall told her, he would buy her the biggest bull in the state of Missouri. In fact, he said, the reason that he asked Hager to get a woman for him was not to have sex, but to mail a letter for him from that city.

At no time, during this period, did Hall fall asleep, and the footlocker and the suitcase remained plainly in view in the room. He did send O'Day out for ice at one point, and it was possible that she made one or more telephone calls.

For his part, Hager was feeling flush, and it appeared that his customer would continue to be generous with him. That day was also his father's birthday, so he arranged to meet his wife—from whom he was separated—in the suburb of Wellston, where at a J.C. Penney's store he bought a shirt, some underwear, and socks for the man he knew as Steve, and a box of cigars for his father. He also explained to his wife that he had a customer who had given him $2,500 for safekeeping, plus $100 for himself, and that his chances looked good that he might make another $400 or $500. Perhaps finally, he hinted, they might even be able to have a decent life for themselves. After leaving his wife in Wellston, he dropped off the cigars for his father, drove to O'Day's house to pick up the clothes she had asked for, and gave her aunt Polly $120.

At 10:30 P.M., Hager reappeared. Hall, clad only in shorts, greeted him at the door and seemed very pleased to see him. They all agreed to have supper together, and to skip going to a nightclub. O'Day wanted to eat at Ruggieri's, a popular restaurant in St. Louis's Italian neighbourhood known as The Hill. Hall refused. While O'Day was putting on her new set of clothes, Hall tried to hand the cabdriver his gun, asking him to keep it for safekeeping. Hager, knowing that it would be disastrous for an ex-convict like himself to be caught with a gun, declined. Instead, he hid the gun in one of O'Day's slippers. All three then went to the Harbor Inn, a small roadside establishment located at 8025 Watson Road, about a mile away. Hall and O'Day ordered steaks, and Hager asked for fried chicken. Hall, worried about the footlocker and suitcase filled with cash that he had left behind at the motel, ate only a few bites. Hager paid the bill.

When all three returned to the Coral Court, Hall, recognizing a kindred spirit in his fellow ex-convict, said to Hager, "You're the right kind of guy." But he seemed unusually fidgety, and asked the cabbie if he could buy him some morphine. Hall also realized that he needed to explain two things—why he had no car and no luggage besides his so-called sample cases; and why he needed morphine. The story he came up with was that his car had been stolen. Also, he was a drug addict, and the stolen luggage contained his drug paraphernalia. Hager replied that he did not know of any place where he could obtain the drug, but that he would try to find some. Hall said that he could easily afford it, and specified that Hager should also get a number 25 or 26 needle for a syringe. He also asked Hager to rent a car in his own name for him, and also to buy a leather suitcase and a briefcase. Hager left sometime around midnight. Hall asked him to return the next day by 10 A.M.

Hall and O'Day had a few more drinks. Finally, they went to sleep. Hall stuffed the keys to his suitcases inside his pillow, and aligned the trunk with the leg of the night table so that he would know if they were moved. He knew there was a risk that O'Day might attempt to roll him.

Hager, according to his own account, drove to Polly Lane's, arriving there around 12:30 A.M. He and Lane were lovers. After an hour, he left, and went to Carrara's Bar at 417 Chestnut Street downtown. Hall had also asked him to procure some bennies. Mary Carrara, the proprietor, got three from Edward Jones, the bellhop of the MacArthur Hotel, which adjoined the bar, and gave them to Hager. Hager then drove to the Lincoln Hotel at 2226 Olive Street and went to bed.

4.

The Third Man

The next morning, Hall and O'Day both awoke around eight. He noticed immediately that the footlocker and the suitcase were in the same spot where he had left them. While waiting for Hager to arrive, they each had a few shots of whisky. As they were moving about, O'Day's elbow bumped against Hall's pillow, and the keys fell out of the pillowcase. When she asked what they were, he merely replied that they were keys, and put them into his pocket. He then asked her to find someone who could bring them something to eat. Strolling out to the balcony of their second-floor room, she spotted a maid and asked her if she could bring them some breakfast. The maid went to her manager to get permission to buy breakfast for the occupants of cabin 49-A, and he bluntly refused.

Hager awoke about the same time as Hall and O'Day, gassed up his cab, and handed his cash receipts from the previous night to Bob James, the dispatcher, telling him about the "angel" he had picked up the previous night. "Angel" was a term used by cabbies, pimps, hookers, and others to indicate a person who spent money lavishly.

Hager also obtained three more bennies from a Black & White Cab driver who happened to be at the lot. After parking his cab, he sought out an Ace mechanic named Chris, giving him $26 for a repair. He then hired a cab to take him to a U-Rent-It agency, where he discovered that no car rental was available that morning. Walking to the Heater Rent-a-Car Company at 365 Olive Street, he rented a two-door green 1952 Plymouth for one day, giving Joseph Costello as a reference. Mildred Binder, the clerk, phoned Costello, who verified the reference. Hager drove to the Ber-Neu Leather Company, a luggage shop at 1810 Washington Street, where he purchased a matching tan leather two-suit bag and a leather briefcase, stating that Costello had directed him to the store. The bill came to $60. He then stopped for breakfast at a restaurant on the same block.

By the time Hager showed up at the Coral Court, between 10:30 and 11:00 A.M., Hall had become extremely agitated. An apologetic Hager explained that he had overslept, and asked whether the police were looking for him.

"No, I think it might be the insurance investigators," Hall replied.

But he was pleased to see Hager, and added that he knew he could count on his new friend. He sent the cabdriver to buy some aspirins, coffee, and fried-egg sandwiches for himself and O'Day.

Hall wanted to put O'Day on a plane to Los Angeles right away with the letter addressed to Patton. After handing her the envelope, he instructed her to mail the letter to Patton immediately upon her arrival. The envelope bore Patton's name and address—1117 Corley Building, St. Joseph, Missouri. Hall then ordered O'Day to step into the bathroom. Opening the suitcase just enough to insert his hand, he withdrew a wad of cash, counted out $1,000 for her expenses, and gave it to her.

After Hall and O'Day had breakfast, he told Hager to drive O'Day to a cab stand in St. Louis where she could catch a cab to the airport, and then to return to the motel to collect him. When Hager asked why Hall could not just ride along with the two of them, Hall replied, "I've got something I want to do."

As soon as Hager and O'Day were on their way back to the city, she told him, "I've got something big to tell you. This guy is loaded with dough. He opened one of the suitcases and there must be a million dollars in it. Don't tell him I told you 'cause he made me swear I wouldn't tell you." Despite Hall's later insistence that neither she nor anyone else had seen the ransom money, O'Day had caught a glimpse of it. While she was sequestered in the bathroom, pretending to take a bath, Hall had opened one of the suitcases. O'Day, gingerly opening the door just a crack, saw it filled with money. She later confronted him, and he—given his almost total lack of insight into either O'Day's or Hager's character—believed her when she promised not to say a word about it. Besides, he figured that she would soon be out of town.

Hager told her to open the envelope and read the letter that Steve, his gullible, free-spending new friend, wanted her to mail from Los Angeles. It read, "Dear Barney, Things are not as good as they seem. I may have to leave the country by ship or plane and when we meet in the future maybe things will be better. Carl."

Hager remarked that he had noticed the initials CAH and the words "St. Joseph, Missouri" on Steve's hatband while his hat lay on the bed. O'Day informed Hager that she was not going to Los Angeles, but to St. Joseph to check up on whoever this Barney Patton was, and try to find out what was going on. Hager asked her to send a telegram to him around eleven that night from St. Joseph, in care of Henry Wilson of the Ace Cab Company, letting him know how she was making out.

While Hager and O'Day were gone, Hall took $20,000 from the black suitcase and put it into the briefcase. He observed that the money looked exactly as it had been when he first placed it there, and that it did not look disturbed.

Learning that the man he knew as Steve was actually named Carl set Hager thinking, specifically, about how to get his hands on more of the money that Steve/Carl—a morphine addict, no less—was so freely handing out. When he returned to the Coral

Court about forty-five minutes later in the rented Plymouth, a very nervous Hall asked him to put the luggage in the car. He left behind the new suitcase Hager had bought for him, but brought along the briefcase filled with $20,000. Hall asked to drive the car himself, but Hager reminded him that, since Hall had no driver's licence, he, Hager, would have to drive. Hall said that he needed to see a man about a dog, and that he also wanted to go to a hardware store—specifying that it be on Route 66, because he did not know the city and wanted to see the Coral Court when he subsequently drove past it. Hager took him to the nearby Hampton Village shopping area, where a Hardware Mart was located.

Hall also asked Hager if he could borrow his cabbie's driver's licence, and Hager told him that he had only a chauffeur's licence with his photo on it. Hall then asked Hager to rent an apartment for him for a month.

"This thing would be fine if it wasn't for this man making the one slip," he said, trying to explain his unusual circumstances and need for secrecy. "That's why I've got to be like this. You know I trust you and Sandy. You don't have to worry. I'm going to really set you up but you've got to play it cool. I need a place in a nice, quiet, refined neighbourhood where I can stay about a month."

Hall even suggested an excuse to explain why he would be staying in a room rented by Hager—that Hager was a dispatcher for Ace Cab, and that his uncle Steve Strand would be staying with him.

Hall also told Hager, "John, if you have no money, you're nothing," and asked for the return of $2,000 of the $2,500 he had given him, and to keep $500 for himself.

But he promised Hager that he would buy him a motel in Florida so that the cabbie would never have to work again, and told him to use the $500 to buy himself a good suit and some shoes—nothing but the best.

He then asked Hager to obtain some bogus identification for him. The cabdriver readily agreed.

Sometime between 1:00 and 1:30 P.M., the two men separated, after agreeing to meet at 4 P.M. at the Pink House. Hall left in the green Plymouth that Hager had rented for him, and Hager caught a cab. On the ride into the city, he wondered if the mysterious errand that his new friend wanted to run was to buy some cartridges for his pistol that O'Day had previously removed. Hager also worried that Hall might steal the car rented in the cabbie's name. Momentarily, he pondered whether he should even call Dick Gerabeck, an officer he knew who worked with the St. Louis Police Department, to tell him about his unusual customer.

But the savvy ex-con quickly dismissed that idea and asked the driver, Howard Hartman, to take him to a tavern on 7th Street downtown. As he continued to mull things over, Hager gradually became convinced that the man with the initials CAH in his hatband was the kidnapper of Bobby Greenlease, and that his footlocker and suitcase contained nothing less than the ransom money. If the cabbie's suspicions were correct, that meant there was only one person he could confide in—not a policeman, not the hooker he occasionally pimped for, but small-time gangster Joe Costello, owner of Ace Cab.

Hall drove to the Hardware Mart in Hampton Village. After telling the clerk, a Mrs. William Koenig, that he wanted to look at garbage cans, he spent three or four minutes studying the display, and then ordered two sixteen-gallon cans. He also asked if she had any large plastic bags. She showed him the store's clothes-dampening bags, measuring about three and a half feet long by one foot wide. Hall asked for four, but the store had only two in stock, which he bought. Appearing to be in a hurry, he also asked for a shovel. Mrs. Koenig showed him a selection, and he chose an ordinary roundnose shovel.

"Well now," he added, "I could use some kind of a plastic spray to protect something. You know what I mean?"

When she showed him a can of Brasco Plastic Spray, he studied it closely, and said, "Fine, I'll take it."

The bill came to $14, and Hall paid it with a $20 bill. He asked Mrs. Koenig to carry the bulky purchases to his car, which she did.

Hall then drove west on Route 66 past the Coral Court, looking for a place to bury the money. He knew that he had to hide it because he was drinking, and that he would not be able to stop—at least not right away. Immediately adjacent to the south side of the motel was a wooded tract of land, approximately twenty-five acres. Also nearby were the ample, partly wooded grounds of Kenrick Seminary, and Resurrection Cemetery, both the property of the Catholic Church. Whether Hall explored either of them is unknown. East of a bridge crossing the Meramec River he saw a road winding around a bluff; but after heading down the road only a short way he became worried that the wheels might get stuck in the muck, and turned back. He recrossed the bridge, took a macadam road, and saw a sign pointing to "Long Beach." He drove back and forth along this road several times, searching for a suitable place to bury the money, but had no luck. A farm that he passed looked ideal for his purposes, but there were several dogs on the property, and he feared they might attack him. Once he got lost and came out on Highway 30 and had to inquire at a filling station how to get back on Route 66. At least one other road led to a dead end. He never left the Plymouth, except once when he stopped to get rid of the garbage cans and other materials in a deserted clubhouse. The odometer showed that he had put only eighty miles on the rental.

Around noon on Tuesday, October 6, soon after Hager dropped off O'Day, a part-time cabdriver for Ace, Herman J. Dreste, got a call from a dispatcher instructing him to pick up a passenger— O'Day—at the Yankee Grill at the corner of Hampton and Oakland, directly across from Forest Park. She gave him $6 and told him to drive her to the TWA ticket office in downtown St. Louis.

"En route she said she had been on a three-day binge," Dreste later recalled, "and had been with a jerk in a county motel." O'Day added that she had been due to be in St. Joseph two days previously, and was scheduled to fly to Los Angeles the next day, when her divorce became final. She also asked Dreste to stop at a store and buy her a bottle of glue because she had a letter that she wanted to seal. Dreste did as she requested.

On the way downtown, though, she asked Dreste if he would drive her to St. Joseph himself, and asked how much the fare might be. "Lady, that's an awful long trip," he replied. "I don't think I can do it." She then asked him to drive her there in his own car, and they agreed on a $150 price. She gave him $80 to buy her some luggage with, claiming that she had lost her own during her drinking binge. She also led the cabdriver to believe that she had two children, was married to a wealthy farmer who lived in New Jersey, and was eager to divorce him.

He dropped her off at her apartment on North 9th Street and waited. O'Day told her aunt Polly to get dressed. They were going to go shopping. After counting out $200 in $10 denominations on a dresser, she gave the money to Lane. Dreste then took them to a Lane Bryant store in downtown St. Louis. There she bought a dark three-piece suit, some grey checked slacks, a blouse, a corset, and some underwear for herself. At a nearby shoe store, she also picked up several pairs of shoes and six pairs of nylons.

While they were shopping, Dreste drove to the Ace Cab garage, where he turned in his cab and the day's receipts. He then drove his own 1949 Chevrolet to downtown St. Louis, bought a suitcase and a matching overnight bag for O'Day, and picked up the two women. Back at their apartment, O'Day packed her clothes, tucked a bundle of $10 bills into a small cosmetics case, and announced that all she had left was $500. She gave her aunt a piece of paper with the name Steve Strand printed on it, along with the address "In care of Western Union, Main Office, St. Louis, Missouri," and on it the message: "Leaving at 2:00 A.M. via TWA, Love, Sandy, 10:00 P.M."

She instructed Lane to be sure to send the telegram to Strand at that address with that exact message at exactly 10 P.M. that night. She told Lane that she was leaving town for two or three days, and not to ask questions, adding that she knew what she was doing and that there was no need for her aunt to worry.

O'Day had no intention of flying to Los Angeles. Once she found out who Steve/Carl really was, she hoped to shake down either him or one of his confederates. She had seen with her own eyes a huge amount of cash, and like Hager, her pimp, she had begun to plot how to get her hands on more of it.

Hager probably had several reasons for suspecting that Hall was hiding something much bigger than fraud. He did not look or act like an executive, banker, or accountant type who might even have the opportunity to embezzle a considerable amount of cash. He was also a drug addict in desperate need of false ID papers. Moreover, according to Hager's later testimony, the two men also revealed that each had once been an inmate in the same penitentiary. Such a disclosure would only have confirmed Hager's growing suspicion that the man named Carl, who currently or only recently lived in St. Joseph, was the probable kidnapper of Bobby Greenlease. Certainly, almost everyone in the country had to be wondering who and where such an individual was—the most wanted man in America. The front-page headlines of all three St. Louis newspapers continued to report the latest developments, including a rumour that a ransom was about to be or had recently been made. All the money Hall was throwing around also suggested a man who had recently come into a very large amount of cash—a ransom perhaps.

As a Missouri native, Hager also knew that St. Joseph was only about an hour's drive from Kansas City, where the kidnapping had taken place. He may even have guessed that the letter Hall wanted O'Day to send to Patton from Los Angeles was designed to throw the police off his scent—a not too difficult surmise. The only other explanation was that he wanted to deceive Patton himself—but the contents of the letter suggested that the two men were friends, not adversaries. The geography, the timing, the two massive trunks presumably packed with money, Hall's paranoid behaviour and request for false ID papers, and perhaps even other clues that Hager managed to pick up—an allusion or reference here and there that the talkative kidnapper might have uttered when he had too much drink—all added up to one thing. Hager had hit the jackpot, and the only way to collect was to confide his suspicions about Hall to his boss and brother ex-convict, Joe Costello.

For Hager's purposes, he was also glad that O'Day—another drunk—had gone off on a quixotic expedition to confront Barney Patton in St. Joseph. With her out of the way, that was just one fewer thing to worry about. If Steve/Carl's two trunks were filled with money, what was the point of going across the state to find more money? Why not just steal what was already there, waiting to be taken?

After cabdriver Howard Hartman dropped Hager off on the corner of 7th and Clark downtown, he drove off, and did not see if Hager actually went into the tavern at the corner. Hager later claimed that he did enter the tavern, changed his mind about calling Sergeant Gerabeck, bought a couple of cigars, and walked north on 7th Street, where he hailed a passing Ace Cab driven by Joe Travis. Travis himself would later testify that Hager did not engage his services on 7th Street, but at the Ace Cab lot at 1835 Washington Avenue, quite some distance away. Most likely, Hager met with Costello at the lot and outlined his suspicions about Hall. He also told the mobster that he had been asked to rent an apartment for Hall in "a nice, quiet, refined neighbourhood." Costello then began to formulate a plan to steal some or all of the ransom.

After getting into the Ace cab, Hager told Travis to take him to the Branscombe Apartments in the Central West End. When he learned that no suitable apartment was available, he strolled over to the nearby Town House Hotel, an apartment annexe of the Congress Hotel, and rented apartment 324 for Hall in his own name.

But Jean Fletcher, the Town House manager, was later to recall that the man she showed apartment 324 to, around 2:30 P.M., wore a business suit, spoke in a cultivated tone, had pink cheeks, and did not have any missing teeth—unlike Hager, who had several teeth missing, spoke poor English, and was not wearing a suit. The man—possibly Costello, who would have followed Hager to the hotel in his own car—paid $185 in cash in advance for a month's rent. The apartment consisted of a living room with two couches, a bath, a kitchen, a bedroom, and French doors opening on to a small porch. Fletcher insisted that she was quite positive that the man who rented the room was neither Hager nor Hall.

After going over their plans for getting together later that evening, Hager and Costello went their separate ways. Hager was in a mood to celebrate. He had $500 in his pocket from Steve/Carl, and he had just done his boss a very big favour—and surely he had reason to believe that Costello would take care of him once he got his hands on the ransom money. Hager was never tempted to steal any of the money for himself because he knew that Costello would soon find out about it. As subsequent events were to prove, Hager also knew that any attempt on his part to steal some of the ransom—the second biggest cash prize in U.S. criminal history*— would also lead to his untimely death.

---

* The Greenlease ransom was the second biggest cash haul in U.S. criminal history, including bank or train robberies, ransom demands, and embezzlement and fraud cases. Three years earlier, on January 17, 1950, a gang of thieves led by Anthony Pino stole $2.7 million from the Brinks Building in Boston. It was easily the largest theft in the annals of crime in America. Of that amount, $1.3 million was in cash, and the rest consisted mostly of cheques and money orders. All eleven members of the gang were eventually arrested, though only $58,000 was recovered. In 1967, twenty-three-year-old mobster Henry Hill stole $420,000 from the Air France air-cargo terminal in New York's JFK International Airport.

Above: Bobby and his governess, Elsie Utlaut, vacationing in Europe.

> *(St. Louis Mercantile Library at the University of Missouri-St. Louis)*

Left: Virginia Greenlease, Bobby's mother.

> *(St. Louis Mercantile Library at the University of Missouri-St. Louis)*

Bobby Greenlease and his father, Robert C. Greenlease.
(St. Louis Mercantile Library at the University of Missouri-St. Louis)

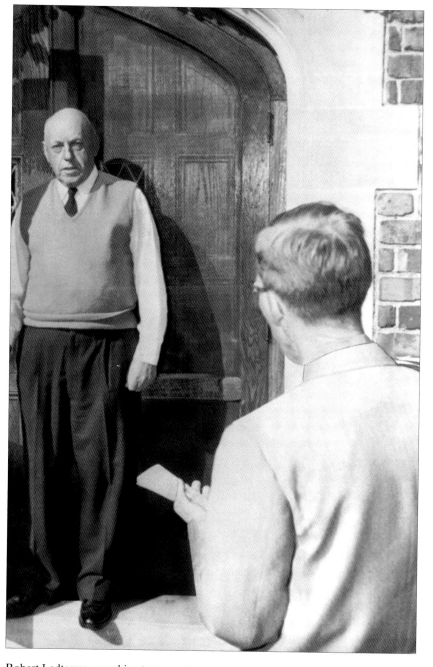

Robert Ledterman speaking to a reporter.

(St. Louis Mercantile Library at the University of Missouri-St. Louis)

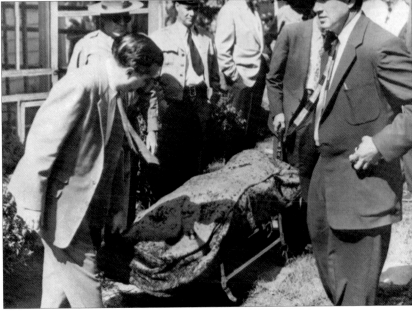

Above: A crowd gathers to watch the unearthing of Bobby's remains behind Heady's home in St. Joseph.

(St. Louis Mercantile Library at the University of Missouri-St. Louis)

Below: The end of a nine-day search.

(St. Louis Mercantile Library at the University of Missouri-St. Louis)

Left: Virginia and Robert Greenlease, and their daughter, Virginia Sue, at the funeral mass for Bobby.

(St. Louis Mercantile Library at the University of Missouri-St. Louis)

Right: Lieutenant Shoulders (left rear) and Patrolman Dolan with Hall and a battered Heady soon after their arrest. Dolan is holding the .38-caliber pistol that Hall used to kill Bobby Greenlease.

(St. Louis Mercantile Library at the University of Missouri-St. Louis)

Above: Heady and Hall soon after their arrest.

> *(St. Louis Mercantile Library at the University of Missouri-St. Louis)*

Below: Prostitute Sandra O'Day, still in handcuffs, after appearing before a grand jury in Kansas City.

> *(St. Louis Mercantile Library at the University of Missouri-St. Louis)*

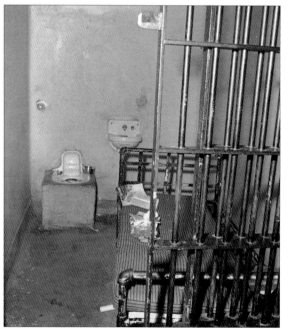

Above: Hall's defence team: R. C. Travis, a family friend; Marshall K. Hoag; Pansy McDowall. Standing: Samuel Tucker.
(Associated Press Images)

Below: Hall's cell on death row.
(Associated Press Images)

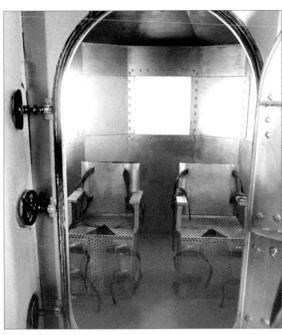

Left: The Missouri gas chamber.

(St. Louis Mercantile Library at the University of Missouri-St. Louis)

Below: Joe Costello bids good-bye to his employees before heading off to prison in 1959.

(St. Louis Mercantile Library at the University of Missouri-St. Louis)

Hager found Travis idling at a nearby cab stand and asked to be taken to the Jarvis Shoe Store at the corner of Grand and Olive. While Travis waited, Hager bought a pair of shoes. He then directed Travis to take him to Boyd's, a downtown clothing store. They drove there directly. While Travis waited in the cab, Hager bought a blue Hickey-Freeman suit for $130, a Dobbs hat for $20, and a belt and buckle set for $90. Presumably, given his straitened circumstances, Hager would not have splurged unless Costello had not assured him of more money to come.

In later testimony, Hager declared that it was at this time—around 3:30 P.M., while he waited for his suit to be altered—that he decided to telephone a policeman he knew named Lieutenant Louis A. Shoulders, and tell him about his suspicions regarding Hall. But Costello and Shoulders were old friends, and Hager's lie was intended only to shield Costello from future police scrutiny.

In Hager's version of events, he went to the nearby Happy Hollow Liquor Store, got a drink, and called Shoulders, saying that he had a customer who was "hot" and was throwing $20 bills around. They agreed to meet, according to Hager, at the corner of Union and Pershing, where the Town House was located, and Hager would lead the lieutenant to Hall.

Hager, according to his later testimony, then said that he returned to Boyd's, at about 4:10 P.M., and picked up his suit. Travis—a Costello employee whose own testimony may also have been dictated by his boss—drove him to the Lincoln Hotel, where Travis waited while Hager changed into his new clothes. Travis then drove Hager to the Pink House to keep his appointment with Hall, arriving there about 4:45.

But it was Costello who contacted Shoulders, who had gone on duty at 3 P.M. that day. Whether they met in person or only talked on the phone is not known. If there was a face-to-face meeting, Hager was also possibly present. The three men may even have met either at the 7th Street tavern or the Ace Cab lot. Shoulders himself violated departmental regulations by not signing in at his precinct when he went on duty at three, claiming he was on a stakeout—a claim that never could be verified. In any case, all three agreed to a plan—to arrest Hall, to keep Costello out of the picture, to grab some of the money, and to make cabdriver John Oliver Hager look like a hero.

And O'Day, Hager assured Costello, would not be around to cause trouble. She was off on a wild-goose chase to St. Joseph.

Around 4 P.M., Hall returned to the vicinity of the Coral Court and mistakenly entered Angelo's restaurant, thinking it was the Pink House, where he was to meet up again with Hager. While drinking a bottle of beer, he groused to the woman behind the bar, "Why can't people keep appointments when they make them?" Ten minutes later, he left, telling the bartender, "If someone comes in asking for Steve, tell him he went home, and he will know what it means." He returned to the motel, waited another quarter of an hour or so, and headed back to Angelo's. This time, though, he realized that the Pink House was across the street, went there, and told someone at the bar to direct a man looking for Steve to go to the motel. Back in his room again, Hall waited for Hager to appear.

Hager, spruced up in his new dark blue suit, dark felt hat, white shirt, and blue-and-white tie, finally did show up in a cab at the Pink House around 4:15 and was given Hall's message. After buying two Dutch Masters cigars, he walked over to the motel and immediately noticed the fresh mud on the tyres and fenders of the rented Plymouth. Hall, for his part, was pleased to see that his friend had bought himself a new outfit.

"You really look sharp," Hall said. "We're going to get a lot of new clothes. We'll even be herding a Cadillac before long. Just take it easy."

Hager handed over the bogus identification that Hall had asked for—a photostat of an Army discharge, a Social Security card, and a medical record, all made out in the name of John J. Byrne, with an address in Kirkwood, a St. Louis suburb. He also told Hall that he had booked a room for him in a nice hotel.

On seeing Hager in his new wardrobe, Hall realized that his own clothes now looked quite soiled by comparison, and he decided to buy himself a new suit as well. The manager of the Pink House told them that several men's stores in the nearby suburb of Clayton were open that evening. In Clayton, the pair found that the Famous-Barr department store was, in fact, closed, but a passer-by informed them that a nearby Boyd's branch was open. Both men went into the store, and Hall told a salesman he needed a new suit immediately. The salesman informed him that the tailors had a backlog of alterations and could not have a new suit ready for him for several days.

"Do you gamble?" Hall asked the salesman. "I'll bet ten dollars you can have a suit ready for me in a day or two."

He gave the salesman $10 and picked out a Hickey Freeman suit for $122. The salesman measured Hall and assured him that the suit would be ready the next day. Hall, who gave his name to the salesman as John Byrne, also purchased a pair of shoes, a Dobbs hat, cuff links, six handkerchiefs, two pairs of socks, a belt, and a tie. While he picked out the shoes, he asked Hager to select six shirts. As they shopped, the store closed. After paying, they started to head back to the Coral Court when Hall remembered that he had asked Hager to rent an apartment for him. Sensing that something might be wrong, he asked him to continue on towards the Coral Court anyway, and drive past. Hager did as instructed, and soon afterwards they stopped at the Villanova Inn, a highway restaurant, for a sandwich and a bottle of beer. Hall was unable to eat, but told Hager to find a woman for him that night for about $200 or $300.

Hager excused himself to make a phone call, ostensibly to arrange for a call girl, but probably to keep Costello apprised of his and Hall's whereabouts. Upon leaving the restaurant, they returned to the Coral Court.

On the way, a nervous Hall said, "When I get hunches, I'd better play them. Something's wrong, we've got to move tonight."

Then he decided not to move to the Town House, after all, so each man started to carry a piece of luggage up to the motel room. Just as they began transferring the luggage, a car pulled up behind Hager's Plymouth. Panicking, Hall told Hager to put the two suitcases back in the trunk. Hager, by now equally spooked, hauled them back to the car and locked them in the trunk. After the other car drove away, Hager explained that the occupants were the people who had rented the room below him.

"I got the shakes," Hall said. "Bad hunch. We've got to move tonight."

They had a drink, and Hall now resolved to move to his new apartment. On the way, they passed through an intersection not far from the apartment where Hall had left Heady, and he remarked, "This looks like the neighbourhood where I parked the car I bought."

Hager replied that he did not know Hall had bought a car. Hall informed him that he had not only bought a car but rented another apartment, but had lost it all—the car, his luggage containing all of his clothes, his identification papers, and his original drug paraphernalia. He again hinted that he might be in trouble with an insurance company. Hager said, "Maybe we can stop and get a paper. Maybe there will be something in there." Hall replied, "No, because it will be handled privately. It may not be heard of."

The previous day, Hall had given Hager an envelope addressed to Esther Grant at 4504 Arsenal. The cabdriver almost certainly passed that information along to Costello as well. Since a woman had taken Bobby Greenlease out of school, the fact that Hall had a woman friend—the name presumably a pseudonym—living in a neighbourhood known for its boarding houses was just another piece of the puzzle fitting into place.

Upon arriving at the Town House apartment, they parked at the side entrance. Hall asked an older man standing at the door to get a bellhop, but instead the man himself unloaded the footlocker and black metal suitcase onto a hand truck, and then Raymond Allen, the bellhop, transported both pieces of luggage, as well as the briefcase, on a pushcart from that point on. There was some confusion about which room was Hall's because many of the rooms were being renovated and had been renumbered. Hall's room, number 324, had formerly been 303. When Allen mistakenly unlocked the wrong door, he discovered that the apartment was occupied.

"What is this?" Hall asked, irritated. "Where's the room?"

Allen apologized for the intrusion. He had to make two trips to the desk downstairs, with Hager accompanying him on one such errand, before he finally obtained the proper key. Hager tipped the bellhop a few dollars, and Hall asked him to bring up two bottles of Coca-Cola. Hager, who was due to leave, ostensibly to procure a call girl, replied that he did not want one. Both men looked about the room, and agreed that it was satisfactory. Before Hager departed, Hall asked him how long he would be gone, and Hager replied that he would be back in about a half-hour or so. When the bellboy returned with the bottle of soda, Hager tipped him another $2. He then left, telling Hall that he would rap three times on the door as a signal that he was back, and say, "Steve, this is John."

The Greenleases may have held out hope that Bobby would be rescued for two reasons. In the previous twenty-one years, the FBI had solved more than 450 kidnapping cases, and had failed to solve only two. Also, kidnapping cases were not usually solved quickly, and in many instances the kidnap victim remained in the hands of abductors for weeks.

On Sunday, October 4, a priest visited the family around noon, remaining about three-quarters of an hour before leaving. The priest returned again on Monday night, around 9:30, and remained until 1:35 in the morning. He returned a third time on Tuesday afternoon; two nuns also appeared at the home that same afternoon to offer comfort.

By October 5, speculation was rife in the newspapers that there would soon be a break in the case. Lending fuel to that rumour was a visit that Arthur Eisenhower, brother of the president, made to the Greenleases. Robert Ledterman had not appeared in his usual role as family spokesman. Asked about Ledterman's whereabouts, Stewart Johnson replied that he had returned to his own home and was napping. Paul Greenlease confirmed to reporters that Ledterman was sound asleep. Meanwhile, the *Chicago American*, a Hearst newspaper, announced on its front page that the kidnapping case had been solved and that an announcement would shortly be made simultaneously in Chicago, Washington, and Kansas City. But Chief Brannon and James A. Robey, the FBI's special agent in charge in Kansas City, firmly stuck to their no-comment guns.

The family slept late on Tuesday, October 6, and at 7:30 A.M. the nurse looking after Mrs. Greenlease arrived. Some reporters had been tipped about the classified advertisement "M: Meet me in Chicago Sunday. G." that had appeared in the *Star*; and rumour now, especially given the *Chicago American*'s apparent scoop, was that Ledterman was in Chicago.

That Tuesday evening, O'Day and Dreste stopped in Columbia, Missouri, where she asked to be taken to a Western Union office, saying she had to send a wire to her lawyer in Los Angeles. They were now en route to St. Joseph on Highway 40, the same highway that Hall and Heady had taken in the early morning hours of the previous day, after picking up the ransom. During the long drive, O'Day—like Hager several hours earlier—tried to collect her thoughts and ponder the fast-moving events of her life in the past twenty-four hours. Her first instinct had been to confront Patton, who was either an embezzler himself, like Hall; or, perhaps, one of the Kansas City kidnappers whose crime was the talk of the nation. As her head cleared and she had time to think, she probably also realized that she had acted precipitately by wanting to go to St. Joseph. Either way, though she had no clear idea of how to proceed, she smelled money, but now her hunch told her to go directly to Kansas City, and to skip St. Joseph. After all, the Greenlease kidnapping had taken place in Kansas City. If Hall was involved, surely she would be able to find out more once she got there. O'Day sent a telegram to her aunt that said: "Hold wire until I contact you. Will advise later. Plans have changed. Don't worry. Love and kisses. Sandy." She did not tell Hager about her change of plans.

As Dreste and O'Day approached the junction of U.S. Highway 71 and U.S. Highway 24, she directed him to head into Kansas City. At a highway tavern, they stopped for a drink, and O'Day asked Dreste for the name of the best hotel in town. He suggested the Hotel Muehlebach, but she also asked the barmaid for her opinion, and she suggested the Hotel President. On calling that hotel, O'Day learned that no rooms were available. Dreste then called the Muehlebach and reserved a room for her. O'Day also told him that she preferred to arrive at the hotel in a cab and not in a private car. By now it was about 9 P.M.

Around this time, Dreste mentioned the Greenlease kidnapping, and O'Day, claiming that she was the mother of two, remarked how horrible it would be if something happened to her children. Dreste agreed, commenting that he had a daughter.

They had a drink at another bar. O'Day then went to a cab stand and got into a cab. That was the last Dreste saw of her. As a precaution, though, he put the $150 that O'Day had given to him into an envelope, and mailed it to his wife. At the Muehlebach, O'Day sent another telegram to her aunt: "Everything fine. Don't worry. Love, Sandy."

When Hager left Hall in his room at the Town House, he simply walked down to the corner of Union and Pershing to await

Shoulders, who arrived at 7:30. He was accompanied by a twenty-five-year-old patrolman, Elmer Dolan. Soon afterwards, Hager phoned Hall to ask if everything was all right, and Hall assured him that it was.

Just moments later, around eight, Hall was sitting in the room alone, drinking whisky. He had also injected a quarter-gram of morphine. When he heard three knocks on the door, he assumed that Hager was delivering the prostitute. The room had a double door that was common in those pre-air-conditioning days—an inner shutter door that allowed ventilation, and a main door opening onto the hallway. Patrolman Dolan gave the message, "Steve, this is John."

As soon as Hall opened both doors, Shoulders and Dolan rushed in. Dolan, the shorter one, was in a police uniform and held a gun on Hall while the taller Shoulders, wearing a double-breasted blue suit, rummaged around the room.

"What the hell is this?" a startled Hall managed to ask. "What's this all about?" His immediate thought was, "The jig is up."

Hall had placed the two pieces of metal luggage in a large closet. Pushed up against the door was the zippered briefcase.

"Be quiet," Shoulders told him. "When I get ready to tell you, I'll tell you. You're under arrest."

"What the hell for?" Hall asked.

Shoulders ordered him to stop asking questions. After frisking Hall, he removed the keys to his luggage from his breast pocket, and instructed Hall to remove his jacket. Dolan told him to sit on an overstuffed chair. Next to that chair was a telephone table containing Hall's now-loaded Smith & Wesson. Hall asked for permission to get himself a drink of whisky, and Dolan told him no. When he asked Dolan what the arrest was all about, Dolan said—quite honestly, in fact—that he did not know.

What Dolan also did not know was that Lieutenant Shoulders, who had commandeered him at the station house on his way out the door because his own partner was off that day, was a shakedown artist who just happened to be an old friend of mobster Joe Costello. Costello and Shoulders had played this game before, though never with such high stakes.

Shoulders went into the closet and unlocked one of the cases. Hall, hearing the lock click open, now repeated aloud what he had suspected just moments before, telling Patrolman Dolan, "I think the jig is up."

"What do you mean?" Dolan asked.

"I don't know what I meant," Hall quickly retorted.

Shoulders said that the police had received a complaint about an unknown man in Hall's apartment who was carrying a gun. Hall thought it odd that the two policemen had ordered him to sit in the overstuffed chair—the perfect place to hide a gun. For that matter, they had not checked the drawer of the telephone table, or anywhere else, to look for a weapon.

Shoulders picked up the briefcase containing about $20,000 and remarked, "You've got a lot of money there, haven't you?"

"Yes, a little bit," Hall agreed.

"What do you do?"

"I'm in the liquor business with my brother," Hall said.

He explained that his brother lived in Illinois, and that, as his forged papers showed, he himself, John J. Byrne, lived in the suburb of Kirkwood.

"I'm going to put the briefcase right back where I found it," Shoulders pointedly told him. "I want you to notice that."

"All right," Hall said.

Shoulders returned it to the exact spot where it had previously lain.

The detective briefly left the apartment—almost certainly to assure Costello, now lurking in the hallway, that the two cases filled with money were still in the closet—and returned moments later. Hall later insisted that, at no time during the ten minutes he was in the room with the two policemen, was anything said about the kidnapping or why he was arrested. Moreover, just prior to their arrival, he had made some notations to himself on an envelope. The calculations represented how many thousands of dollars he had removed from the two suitcases in the closet, and he estimated that he still had between $560,000 and $570,000. On the other side of the envelope, he had jotted down a list of several items of clothing he planned to purchase the following day.

When the two policemen accompanied Hall out of the room, they locked the door, leaving the two suitcases and the briefcase behind. Hall was still not entirely sure what was happening. But he did have enough of his wits about him, as the last man to leave the apartment, to notice that the two brass keys to the footlocker were still lying on the dresser. The black key to the smaller suitcase, which Shoulders had taken from him, was missing. Hall was quite positive—both then and later—that neither piece of luggage was taken out of the room at that time.

Shoulders advised Hall that he was going to be taken to a police station through the hotel's rear stairway so that, if nothing was the matter, he could return without having been embarrassed before the other guests. The ruse was obviously calculated to avoid having anyone witness the arrest. As Dolan led him down the corridor, Hall glanced back and observed Shoulders talking to a very slender man of medium height in the middle of the hallway. The man was wearing a light tan snap-brim hat, and a pair of rust-coloured slacks with a matching short jacket gathered at the belt line—a so-called Eisenhower jacket. When Dolan and Hall reached the end of the corridor, they discovered that there was no rear stairway. They rejoined Shoulders. By now, the mysterious third man had disappeared.

Shoulders, Dolan, and Hall then descended another stairway, exited through the back door, and walked around the side of the building. Near the side entrance, Hall observed a parked automobile with the interior light on and a woman with short blond hair sitting inside. The three men walked to the front of the apartment building to an unmarked police car parked on the side of the Congress Hotel. All three sat in front, with Dolan driving, and Hall in the middle. They drove directly to the police station, about ten minutes away.

The two policemen had not put Hall in handcuffs, nor mentioned the kidnapping, and he still did not know why he had been arrested. Shoulders, after all, had merely alluded to someone complaining about a hotel guest with a gun. Dolan, too, had seemed befuddled about why Hall was being arrested. What Hall did know, though, was that he had left behind two pieces of luggage containing nearly $600,000. With a sense of sickening doom, he also realized that Hager, his good pal, had double-crossed him, and that his fantasy world was about to crash and burn.

5.

The Shadow

The Newstead Avenue police station in the Central West End where Shoulders and Dolan brought Hall in for questioning was a sturdy, turn-of-the-century, three-storey red-brick building bordered on either side by a popular neighbourhood bar, Jimmy and Andy's, and an alley. Hall had repeatedly glanced at his watch, while waiting for Hager to appear, and was quite adamant in later testimony that he, Shoulders, and Dolan had left the Town House apartment at 8:15 P.M. The two policemen, however, insisted that they left the apartment at 8:30.

When Hall, escorted by Shoulders and Dolan, arrived at the station, he gave his name to the acting desk sergeant, Corporal Raymond Bergmeier, as John J. Byrne. Bergmeier was later to testify that, when Hall was booked at 8:57 P.M., he did not see Shoulders, Dolan, or Hall carry any suitcases into the station. After Hall was searched, his personal items were taken from him, including his wristwatch, a Papermate ballpoint pen, a cigarette lighter, and about $700 in cash. He was given a receipt and

Shoulders escorted him to the holdover cells, telling the guard on duty, Lyle Mudd, to put him into a cell by himself.

When he was alone, Hall called Mudd and said to him, "I want to make a phone call."

"I haven't got the booking sheets back," Mudd replied.

"Where's the big fellow that brought me in?" Hall asked. "I want to see him. I want to talk to him."

"Do you mean that?" Mudd asked.

"You match me up with the gun, and you'll get $2,000," Hall told him. "I've got the money. I've got $20,000, and I'll give you $2,000 to get me in touch with that fellow right away." He added that he would also give $5,000 to Shoulders if he would agree to talk to him.

"Who do I have to kill?" Mudd said, jokingly.

"You get me in touch with him," Hall said, "and you'll get your dough."

"All right," Mudd said. "I'll do my best."

Hall was desperate to talk to Shoulders because he was still not absolutely sure why he was being charged, and was anxious to the point of nervous collapse about the money left behind in the hotel room. In his near-delirium, he also held out hope that perhaps he could bribe his way out of his hopeless predicament. Unable to ignore Hall's persistent and increasingly frantic demands to talk to the detective who arrested him, Mudd finally told him, "I've given Shoulders three bells," meaning that he had asked the police lieutenant to drop everything and come. "If that doesn't get him, I don't know what to do."

Shoulders, though, had other priorities than talking to the most wanted man in America. His movements and whereabouts, and those of Dolan, immediately after bringing Hall to the police station were to forever become the subject of intense speculation and scrutiny by the FBI, the St. Louis Police Department, and the press—and added yet another layer of greed, contempt for the rule of law, and indifference to the suffering of Bobby's family in the Greenlease case.

As time passed, Mudd did give Hall one clue to what was happening when he remarked, "We got a hell of a lot of money out front."

Lost in a hellish funk, Hall said nothing. For two hours, he remained alone in the holdover cell, while slowly going through severe alcohol and morphine withdrawal.

Some years prior to Hall's arrest, Shoulders and Costello had both been cabdrivers for the taxi company that the latter now owned. Over the years, they had shaken down any number of petty criminals, always splitting the proceeds fifty-fifty. Shoulders, known as "the Shadow," was considered a courageous policeman, who had killed two men in the line of duty—though, according to some, the circumstances surrounding both deaths were questionable. He was also suspected of receiving payoffs from brothel owners and gambling dens.

Often in the news, Shoulders first achieved local fame in 1937 after he pursued and fatally wounded Alvin Mott, an escaped Michigan convict who had killed a policeman. Shoulders gained his reputation as the Shadow for his practice of prowling through back yards and alleys in search of policy operators and other wrongdoers while making his rounds. He was promoted to lieutenant in 1942, and later boasted of refusing to take a bribe from Joseph Newell, a labour boss whose stepson was in trouble with the law. Shoulders and Newell were friends who visited each other's homes. The stepson subsequently shot and killed Newell.

As the case against Hall progressed, Shoulders's shady reputation, combined with Hall's own dubious record as a petty thief turned kidnapper, were to leave the FBI and the St. Louis Police Department in a quandary. Whom to believe about the events surrounding Hall's arrest: the corrupt detective or—improbably—the psychopathic child murderer he arrested? More lies, cover-ups, and layers of intrigue were still to come that would only further complicate the FBI's investigation. Caught in the middle of the most sensational crime St. Louis had ever known was Elmer Dolan, a young patrolman with an impeccable record.

In the fabricated version of events told by Shoulders and Dolan, they not only delivered Hall to the station, but they also brought with them at the same time the green footlocker, the small black metal suitcase, and the briefcase that they assumed were stuffed with the entire ransom amount. Shoulders later declared that, as they were leaving the hotel room, he carried the small black metal suitcase to the door. He then motioned for Hager, who had come forward, to take it downstairs and place it in the police car. Dolan, who was carrying the briefcase, guarded Hall, while Shoulders followed behind, lugging the green footlocker and locking the door. The two policemen and Hall then drove to the Newstead station, with Hager tailing them in his own car. When Shoulders, Dolan, and Hall arrived at the station house, Dolan allegedly reached into the rear of the car, picked up the briefcase and the black metal suitcase, and for the first time noticed the footlocker placed there by Hager on Shoulders's instructions. Dolan then carried the black suitcase and briefcase up the steps of the station, just steps behind Shoulders and Hall, and deposited both on the floor of Shoulders's office. While Hall was being booked, Shoulders stepped outside to retrieve the footlocker.

Hager, meanwhile, allegedly was to wait in a courtyard in the rear of the station for nearly an hour until summoned by Shoulders into his office.

Shoulders said that, after returning to his office with the footlocker, he opened the briefcase and discovered an insurance card with the name Carl A. Hall printed on it with his St. Joseph address. Putting the card in his pocket, he forced open the two suitcases, found that both were only partly full, and put both into his private locker, which he locked. Dolan claimed he witnessed Shoulders putting the luggage into his private locker.

No witness observed either Dolan or Shoulders bringing a

suitcase into the station house, however. Moreover, within the hour both Shoulders and Dolan separately left the precinct, claiming they had personal errands to run.

In fact, what most law enforcement officials ultimately came to believe happened, but could not prove, was that Costello was the third man in the hotel corridor whom Hall had glimpsed as Dolan escorted him to the unmarked police car. Ex-convict and Costello employee John Hager's enormous lie—that he had tipped Shoulders about the free-spending Hall, when he had actually called Costello—further obstructed the police investigation into the missing ransom.

After they put Hall into a holdover cell, Shoulders and Dolan had actually raced back to the Town House. Witnesses observed three men, around 9 P.M., hurriedly carrying luggage from the hotel's north entrance on Pershing Street to a parked car. Two of the men—probably Dolan and Hager—put the footlocker into one car and drove off, heading for Costello's home in South St. Louis. The third man—who, like Shoulders, wore a dark suit and horn-rimmed glasses—drove off in a second car with the black metal suitcase, and briefly stopped to make an appearance at the Newstead station.

About 9:30, Shoulders left the station again, without reporting his absence. He later testified that he wanted to go home to turn his private car over to his so-called landlady, June Marie George, since he would be working on the case into the wee hours. While Shoulders was heading home, Dolan—who was in a radio car—heard a call put out for the lieutenant by Mudd, the jail guard. Mudd informed Dolan that Hall insisted on talking to Shoulders immediately. Dolan contacted Shoulders and then called the station back, saying, "We have found the money. Everything is under control. Forget about it."

Shoulders then joined Dolan, Hager, and Costello in the

basement of the latter's modest home on Gurney Court, a U-shaped side street that opened onto Tower Grove Park. The entire ransom, minus what Hall had spent, was stacked on a table, and Shoulders offered Dolan $50,000 in hush money.

"I don't want anything to do with that crap," Dolan said.

"You really don't have anything to say about it," Shoulders menacingly replied.

Dolan, a married man and father of several young children, got the message.

Across the park, Heady was still holed up in the apartment on Arsenal Street.

When Shoulders, Dolan, and Hager left Costello's house, the lieutenant instructed the two other men to return to Hall's room at the Town House and search it. They did so, finding the Smith & Wesson, a bottle of whisky, and some clothes, which Dolan brought to the Newstead station. Shoulders returned there directly. Hager later helped him to smuggle in Hall's luggage by parking a car in the dark alley next to the station and passing the two pieces through a window. At 10:40 P.M., Shoulders put out a call for two special officers—detectives who were to be assigned a specific task. Soon afterwards, almost two hours after he had booked Hall, the lieutenant confronted his prisoner, saying, "There's a lot of money out there, isn't there?"

"Yes," Hall said.

"You're wanted in that kidnapping, aren't you?" Shoulders persisted.

Hall tried to evade the accusation as best as he could. But Shoulders told him, "We can't hold this up much longer from the FBI."

Knowing that it was useless to continue the masquerade, Hall said, "That's right."

Shoulders left Hall for about ten minutes—perhaps to confer with Costello once again, by phone or in person, and confirm that the money they had taken from Hall was indeed part of the Greenlease ransom. When the detective returned, he again confronted Hall.

"What's the whole story?" he demanded. "Tell me, and I'll get a promotion out of it."

While sitting in the cell, Hall had not only come to the abysmal conclusion that his dream of living the good life in La Jolla was over. He also had just enough presence of mind to realize that he would be charged with both kidnapping and murder once the body of Bobby Greenlease was found. In a desperate bid to save his life, he hurriedly concocted a story that he hoped just might get him a sentence of life imprisonment instead of the death penalty. Just as there had been a mysterious third man who was the accomplice of Shoulders and Dolan, Hall created a fictitious third party to the kidnapping. His name was Tom Marsh. Hall knew no one by that name; it simply came to him.

In his fevered plotting, he created a profile of Marsh as a tattooed sex degenerate, predatory child molester, and drug addict who had been responsible for looking after Bobby once he was taken from the school. In this version of events, Hall—and Heady—had every intention of returning the boy to his parents once the ransom was collected. Hall even, in a moment of perverted gallantry, decided to try to save Heady by resurrecting the lie that he had used to recruit her in the first place—insisting that he had duped her into believing that Bobby was his son from an earlier marriage. Such was the story he told Shoulders.

Shoulders again left Hall on his own. About fifteen minutes later, he returned and demanded to know the whereabouts of the woman who took Bobby from the school. Since it was likely that he already knew the address, Shoulders needed to make it appear that he was following proper procedure. After Hall gave up the address, Shoulders dispatched four special officers to arrest Heady. These included the two he had requested earlier that evening, Edward Bradley and Norman Naher. Two other special officers,

William Carson and Lawrence King, joined them. After handcuffing Hall, the four officers left the station with the suspect to arrest Heady. Departing from the station around 11:30 P.M., they soon arrived at the Arsenal Street apartment, and altogether were gone about an hour and a half—much to Shoulders's annoyance, because they interrogated Hall at the apartment and did not immediately return to the station. Heady was taken to the precinct and booked at approximately 1 A.M. on Wednesday, October 7.

Heady, after Hall dumped her, had remained at the apartment except for a brief excursion at five on Tuesday evening, when she took a cab to the Old Shillelagh Bar, where she downed two shots and bought a fifth of whisky. At a nearby store, she also bought milk and a newspaper, and then immediately returned to the apartment. She discovered the $2,500 Hall left for her only when rummaging in her purse to pay for her purchases, but decided not to use any of that money. Also in her purse was her .25 calibre revolver.

At the time of her arrest, Heady had a large bruise on her forehead over her right eye and an abrasion on the bridge of her nose, where Hall had punched her. A woman who often went for days without eating, she was also suffering from acute alcoholism, and could remember very little about the kidnapping.

St. Louis police also quickly recovered the Nash that Hall had purchased and immediately abandoned.

While the special agents, accompanied by Hall, were proceeding to arrest Heady, Shoulders contacted St. Louis chief of police Jeremiah J. O'Connell at his home and informed him that he had apprehended the kidnapper of Bobby Greenlease. O'Connell immediately left for the station, and was joined a short time later by agents of the Federal Bureau of Investigation. After Shoulders showed them the suitcases that he claimed Hall had with him at the time of his arrest, the money was counted, and it was ascertained that half the ransom money was missing. Costello and his cohorts had kept $303,720 for themselves. Only $296,280 was recovered.

At two o'clock on Wednesday morning, Hall was taken to a room at the police station, vomiting and groaning. Up until this point, he had confessed only to kidnapping Bobby, but not to killing him. Sticking to the story that he hastily devised in the holding cell, he admitted that he knew Bobby's older, adopted brother, Paul, from having attended military school with him. "I knew the family was wealthy and thought of kidnapping him for about two years and planned it on several occasions," he said.

Heady, he said in a signed statement, believed that Bobby "was my son and that my former wife did not want me to see him. I told her to tell the nun or the person who answered the door to say that Bobby's mother was ill and that she had come for him." After Heady returned with Bobby to the Katz parking lot, according to Hall, he dropped her off at Country Club Plaza, promising to return within an hour. He then drove the boy to Westport Road, where he turned him over to their partner Tom Marsh, who was to take him to Heady's home in St. Joseph. Marsh, Hall said, was driving a gunmetal grey 1950 Chevrolet.

By happenstance, Heady overheard two police officers discussing Hall's fictitious version of the kidnapping and slaying of Bobby Greenlease. She heard enough that she quickly blamed the murder on Marsh, and absolved herself of kidnapping and murder charges by insisting that Hall told her the boy was his son from a previous marriage.

In a further elaboration of his story about the nonexistent Tom Marsh, Hall said that they had met in the bar of the Netherlands Hotel in Kansas City. Hall immediately discerned that Marsh was an ex-convict from his use of certain slang expressions used by prison inmates, and invited him to join in the kidnapping. During their planning, Hall further alleged, he gave Marsh the .38 calibre Smith & Wesson, which Marsh requested for his own protection in the event that he was stopped while looking after Bobby.

During his interrogation by the FBI, Hall identified himself as an insurance agent. Several times during the interview, he slipped out of his chair. He was also perspiring heavily, and he vomited so often that someone said, "Get something for him to puke in." Hall continued to vomit into a wastebasket. The FBI was not sure whether Hall's condition was the result of alcohol poisoning or the effects of the morphine wearing off. Most of Hall's replies to questions put to him were yeses or inarticulate. Just before 3 A.M., he passed out.

An ambulance took Hall to City Hospital, where Dr. Cecil Auner diagnosed him as suffering from acute alcoholism. Auner said that Hall was "semi-comatose [and] crying and mumbling for water." He described Hall as being "very depressed" and unable to answer questions about his physical condition. Auner gave him caffeinated sodium benzoate as a stimulant.

Hall finally recuperated enough to tell the doctor that he was a morphine addict, and had taken a quarter of a gram orally, but he added that he never took more than that amount at any one time. Even though Hall had asked Hager to bring him a syringe and needle, Auner found no needle marks or other evidence of drug addiction.

After Hall revived somewhat, he was taken back to the station and the interrogation continued, though he was able to give little more than a mumbled and inarticulate account of his whereabouts for the past few days in St. Louis. Finally, he recovered enough to tell the FBI that Bobby should have been released in Pittsburg, Kansas, by Marsh, who had the responsibility of taking care of the child.

Under relentless questioning, Hall finally admitted that Bobby was dead and had been buried in Heady's back yard in St. Joseph. Yet his attempt at a cover-up continued. After picking up Heady at Country Club Plaza in her Plymouth station wagon, he now said, they drove to her home, where he discovered that Marsh had killed Bobby. He buried Bobby's body in the backyard after removing the religious medal, which he subsequently sent to the Greenlease family in his note.

Q. Was he dead when you got there?
A. Yes.
Q. Where was the other man?
A. He was gone.
Q. How was he killed?
A. With a gun.
Q. Where was he shot?
A. I don't remember. I don't even know.
Q. What did you do when you found him in this condition?
A. I had to bury him.
Q. Where did you bury him?
A. In the backyard.

By extraordinary coincidence, the FBI had on file a name—Thomas John Marsh—that matched that of Hall's fictitious associate. When agents showed Hall a photograph of Marsh, he would neither identify nor disavow that particular Marsh as his fellow kidnapper. Newspapers around the world, however, played up the manhunt for the real Marsh on their front pages, characterizing him as a tattooed sex degenerate who had eighteen arrests on his record. The real Tom Marsh had once been arrested in St. Louis, in 1950, and charged with a sex offence involving an eight-year-old boy, and later served five years in the Oklahoma State Penitentiary. According to FBI files, his left ring finger had been amputated at the joint, and a tattoo on his right forearm bore the inscription "In memory of sister—Tom Marsh."

Acutely aware of the numerous implausibilities and inconsistencies in Hall's confession, FBI agents pressured him to admit that he did not have an accomplice named Tom Marsh; and to admit that he, Carl Austin Hall, murdered Bobby. But Hall emotionally denied that claim, even while declaring, "I know that I'm going to die, and that I am more responsible than anyone else because I planned the kidnapping and it resulted in the death of Bobby Greenlease."

Repeated questioning resulted in repeated denials, as he continued to insist, over and over, "I didn't do it. I didn't do it. I didn't do it." Rather, he said, Marsh was the one who killed Bobby, most likely in Heady's basement. He said he had bought the lime poured over Bobby's body two or three months earlier from a lumberyard because Heady wanted to revitalize the soil before planting tomatoes. When the FBI pointed out that tomatoes were normally planted in the spring, Hall replied that he was merely heeding Heady's desire to plant some in the late summer months.

Bail for both Hall and Heady was set at $100,000 each, or about $1.5 million each in today's money.

Around 4:30 A.M., police reporter John Kinsella, a big, friendly Irishman who worked for the *St. Louis Post-Dispatch*, showed up at police headquarters on 12th Street downtown. A veteran newspaperman, he immediately sensed something in the air, a buzz. Before long, he learned that Chief O'Connell and an FBI agent had gone to the Newstead Avenue station in the middle of the night, and that they were still there. Most of the cops were Kinsella's pals, but this time no one would tell him what was happening. Kinsella alerted his city editor, Raymond Crowley, who dispatched a reporter, James A. Kearns, Jr., to the Newstead station. Kearns quickly discovered that Hall and Heady had been arrested, and thought that he had a scoop, since he was the only reporter on the premises. But forty-five minutes later a swarm of reporters and radio and TV people rushed in, summoned by the police. All were brought into an office, where Hall and Heady were put on display as the kidnappers of Bobby Greenlease. A spokesman for the police department also announced that half of the ransom money was still missing.

At some point, Heady asked to go to the rest room. An FBI agent asked the receptionist, June Michael, to accompany Heady to make sure that she did not try to harm herself. Heady was weeping and mumbling, and in the bathroom said to Michael, "You know, he put his little hand in mine, and he was so trusting."

Kansas City police arrested Sandra O'Day at 4:45 A.M. that morning in her room at the St. Regis Hotel, just forty-five minutes after she checked in. Upon arriving in the city, she had gone to a bar for a drink, fell in with a group of patrons, and joined them in a series of bar hops. Sharing her bed at the time of her arrest was another prostitute.

That same Wednesday morning, Hall was transferred to the City Jail downtown. Throughout his interrogation, he had not wavered on two key points: that neither Shoulders nor Dolan had asked him if he had a gun, even though a loaded .38 (the very one, of course, that he had allegedly given to Marsh) was in his telephone table drawer; and that he had not seen either the footlocker or metal suitcase from the time of his arrest. He remained quite emphatic that neither Shoulders nor Dolan carried any luggage to the car. Each had a hand on his elbow from the time they left the hotel until they got into the car, except for the brief time when Shoulders spoke to the mysterious third man in the corridor. He insisted that he had never opened the large metal footlocker after he originally filled it with the contents of the duffel bag, and had kept the keys to both cases in his possession until he was arrested. Further, he stated that he had opened only the smaller trunk on two occasions at the Coral Court, and at no point did either piece of luggage seem lighter than it had previously.

Heady at first was confused with another Heady who had been arrested in 1933 on prostitution charges in Danville, Illinois, and in Kansas City in 1935 on suspicion of being involved in a robbery, and also that same year for helping a prisoner to escape.

The vigil for Bobby ended very late Tuesday evening, or in the early hours of Wednesday morning. About seventy-five reporters and photographers from wire services, newspapers, national magazines, radio, and television were gathered outside the Greenlease home when a man passing by in his car announced that he had just heard a news bulletin over the radio that police had learned that Bobby Greenlease was dead. The newsmen rushed en masse to the door of the Greenlease home and asked the nurse who answered if they could speak to Ledterman. He appeared and said that the family had received no word about the police report. Moments later, he reappeared, walked slowly down the circular drive, as was his custom, and spoke to the reporters again. "The FBI has informed us that it is true," he said. "That is all now." Then he slowly walked back to the house.

Within minutes, telegrams began arriving. The messenger handed them to a policeman, who took them to the front door. The stunned reporters gathered around two car radios to hear the latest word on the kidnapping. Since much of the news was coming from FBI headquarters, the newsmen had to depend on the radio and, soon afterwards, copies of extra editions of the *Star* to file their own stories.

Later, a man and a woman left the Greenlease home with Bobby's sister, Virginia Sue. The man carried a suitcase, and presumably Bobby's sister was being sent away for a few days.

At ten on Wednesday morning, the FBI formally announced that the body of Bobby Greenlease was found in a shallow grave at the rear of a home in St. Joseph, that two of his abductors were being held, and that a nationwide dragnet was being mounted for a third suspect named Thomas Marsh. The agency also confirmed that the family had paid a ransom of $600,000, and that about half of it was missing.

A half-hour later, Ledterman and O'Neill appeared in front of the Greenlease home, and announced that they had made contact with the kidnappers at approximately 12:05 on the previous Sunday morning, but declined to elaborate.

"But a man has confessed he killed the boy, so that is what it is," Ledterman said, in an apparent reference to the fictitious Marsh. Hall had still not confessed to the murder. "We did all we could to get the boy back."

Around 3 A.M., Kansas City FBI agent Richard Martin received a phone call telling him to go to Heady's house and begin the search for Bobby Greenlease's body. He and another agent entered through an unlocked bedroom window, and soon discovered blood on the floor of the basement garage. Going into the back yard, they used their flashlights to find the wilting chrysanthemums planted over Bobby's grave. They then set about securing the area. Around dawn, a workman named Claude James walked by, and the two agents hired him to begin the digging.

It was a perfect autumn morning, with the wind gently rippling through the leaves of the maple and elm trees in front of the house. The grave was located on the north side of the porch of Heady's white house. A blacktop road passed in front, while the side street, Penn, was gravel. The white mailbox in front identified the owner as Bonnie Brown Heady. By ten o'clock, several hundred onlookers had crowded around to watch, and traffic on nearby roads was bumper to bumper. Only a honeysuckle hedge and ropes stretched along the road by the highway patrol kept them back. A few morbidly obsessed onlookers, not to be denied, brought ladders, while others lay on their stomachs in an attempt to peer under the hedge. Some even looked down from nearby rooftops. Neighbours described Heady as a quiet woman who kept to herself. No one could recall seeing her in the past week or so, and several local newspapers, still rolled up and tied with string, were scattered haphazardly on the gravel driveway.

Slowly, James began digging in an area measuring about four by six feet, gently scooping away the top dirt bit by bit. Withered flowers that had been blooming only days earlier were now mixed with the dirt and lime. About an hour later James reached the lime, which was about a foot beneath the surface. Bobby had been placed in the grave on his back, with the used lime sack thrown near his feet. Two undertakers, their pants legs rolled up, stepped into the grave, lifted the blue-shrouded corpse to the surface, and placed it on a white sheet. After the corpse was wrapped in the sheet, it was put on a stretcher, removed to an ambulance, and taken to the Meierhoffer-Fleeman Chapel. The blue shroud was not opened at the scene.

Waiting for the ambulance bearing Bobby's body were Buchanan County coroner H. F. Moody and Dr. Hubert Eversull, the Greenlease family dentist. Bobby had visited the dentist shortly before going on the European vacation with his family. Dr. Eversull had brought Bobby's chart, which showed six cavities, and positively identified the remains as Bobby's. His body was badly decomposed, and his face all but obliterated.

The police also searched the basement where Bobby had been laid before he was buried. Despite Hall's efforts to scour away all traces of the body, bloodstains were found on the floor beneath the steps leading down to the basement, on a fibre mat on the back porch, and on the handle of the screen door. The police also discovered bloodstains on Heady's nylon blouse. A photograph of the basement garage published in *The Kansas City Star* showed a large oil stain from the station wagon on the floor; chicken wire that Heady had placed around the furnace to keep her boxer away from the hot metal; and a bushel basket containing several whisky bottles.

The FBI laboratory later ascertained that a lead bullet recovered from a rubber floor mat in Heady's Plymouth station wagon had also been fired from Hall's Smith & Wesson.

On Wednesday afternoon, Dr. Fred B. Kyger visited the Greenlease home, and remained about forty-five minutes. When he left, there were tears in his eyes.

"I was here just as a friend of the family," he told reporters, "and not on a professional visit. My wife and I had dinner with Mr. and Mrs. Greenlease the night before Bobby disappeared, and I delivered both of their children. Mrs. Greenlease is obviously disturbed about the events. That is about all I can tell you."

Heady's neighbour, Mrs. J. F. Hesselmeyer, was incredulous. "I used to call on her for Red Cross and Community Chest donations," she said, "and she always gave."

In Pleasanton, everybody was in disbelief that Zella Hall's son had been involved in the kidnapping. Marsh Bradley, publisher of the *Pleasanton Observer-Enterprise*, said, "Everybody was just dumbfounded. They just couldn't believe that a home-town boy had a part in the fiendish crime they had been reading and hearing so much about."

Paul Greenlease, shown a photograph of his former classmate, remarked only, "He looks vaguely familiar."

6.

Burial

The Greenlease family, their friends, many of Bobby's schoolmates, and hundreds of sympathetic Kansas Citians offered solemn tribute to his memory at three religious services on Friday, October 9. The first was held at the Stine & McClure Chapel, where everyone simply knelt in silent prayer. Not a word was spoken. The funeral cortege then made its way to St. Agnes Church. Four pallbearers—Norbert O'Neill, R. T. Moore, attorney E. R. Morrison, and Robert Ledterman—guided the casket adorned with flowers to the foot of the altar. Virginia and Robert Greenlease, other members of the family, and close friends followed behind. Every seat in the church was taken, and the aisles and front steps were also crowded with people. About fifty of Bobby's classmates from the French Institute sat on both sides of the church, while about twenty-five priests knelt in the sanctuary.

Archbishop Edward J. Hunkeler, prelate of the Kansas City diocese in Kansas, presided over the "mass of angels"—a requiem so called because it was often celebrated for children, with the altar decorated in white instead of the traditional black for adults.

The Reverend Joseph M. Freeman, SJ, of Rockhurst College served as the assistant priest. A children's choir comprised of students from St. Agnes Church sang throughout the service.

In his sermon, Archbishop Hunkeler told the congregation that Bobby's suffering had been Christ-like. Directly addressing the family, who were seated in the front row, the prelate said, "Your sorrow is not in that the cheery person is gone. But in the agonizing fear that he was in the hands of evil persons." He closed with the words: "His soul was blessed by God. Therefore, He has hastened to take it."

At the end of the service, everyone stood on the church lawn with heads bowed as the funeral procession started for Forest Hills Cemetery. Upon arrival at the cemetery, the casket was carried up a long flight of stone steps to the abbey chapel, where about fifty family members and friends formed a circle for a brief "burial service for children" in the stone rotunda. Baskets of flowers were banked against the grey marble walls. The abbey contained only seven crypt rooms, and the Greenlease family had arranged for one only after Bobby's death. Its doorway was draped in red velvet and tied with gold cords. The service began with a reading of Psalm 148, a song of praise, which in the Douay-Rheims translation used at the time began:

> Praise ye the Lord from the heavens: praise ye him in the high places.
> Praise ye him, all his angels: praise ye him, all his hosts.

After a brief prayer, Bobby was interred in the crypt and the last of the mourners left the abbey. Shortly after the service, Robert Greenlease stood outside the family home and issued a statement expressing his appreciation to the Kansas City press and other news media, and to the Kansas City Police Department, for their cooperation.

"We want to thank the press, especially *The Kansas City Star*, for its fair cooperation in respecting family wishes in matters we could not discuss during the time of this trying ordeal," he said. He specifically thanked photographer Dave Cauthen and reporter Franklin S. Riley, Jr. Referring to the Kansas City Police Department, he thanked it for showing "a willingness to go along with us in things we couldn't have gotten on without." By that he meant that he was grateful that the family was allowed to do whatever it thought best in its attempt to get Bobby back. He also thanked the city's banks for their cooperation, and offered his "sincere appreciation" to the family's many friends. "At times," he said, his voice trembling, "I know we were rude, short, and curt to our dear friends." Also included in the litany of thanks were the hundreds of people who had sent letters and telegrams of support, even from as far away as Cuba, France, Germany, and Italy, and to the many "fine neighbours" who permitted the use of their telephones and frequently fed the press waiting outside the Greenlease home.

Many newspapers around the nation devoted front-page coverage to Bobby's funeral, and it was featured in a heartbreaking, two-page spread in *Life*. Some papers also published editorials condemning, in the strongest possible terms, the murder of an innocent boy, and expressing an inability even to comprehend the scale of depravity that the kidnappers had displayed. One of the most eloquent, and outraged, appeared in *The New York Times*:

The Kidnapping

Most of us lead sheltered lives, in the sense at least that among the people we know and even meet casually there operates a relatively high moral conscience. Whom do we know that would torture an animal, kill a child? Thus when a crime of almost incredible inhumanity comes before us, like the kidnapping and murder of 6-year-old Bobby Greenlease, we are struck dumb. When extreme cruelty is perpetuated by single individuals we tend, most of us, to lay the thing to a deranged mind. But when several persons conspire to snatch a child from his parents, put a bullet through his head, and then go on to torture the parents for days, we go wanting for an answer to the reasoning that underlies the crime. One can look among the ways of the wildest beasts and not find parallels to such avariciousness, cunning and gratuitous cruelty.

Laid bare now are the histories of these people. It is a tale of drink and depravity, of police records and prison walls, in which the prime mover is a rich man's son who squandered an inherited fortune and turned to crime, his latest being the most terrible and sickening of all. But even given such personal lives, still one is forced against the wall for an explanation to the mental processes and rationalizations of this kidnapping and slaughter.

There never seems much point after the deed is done to speak out vindictive stricture against the guilty. But this crime is so heinous, so contrary to all human feeling, that no punishment the civilized laws of this land allow seems quite adequate.

On Saturday, October 10, the day after Bobby's burial, the St. Louis Police Department launched an intensive search for the missing ransom money. At the unofficial level, hundreds and perhaps thousands of St. Louisans were also combing the city, hoping to find the money and, presumably, to turn it over for a reward. Popular hunting grounds included the 1,293 acre Forest Park, site of the 1904 World's Fair. Only a few blocks from the Town House apartment where Hall had been arrested, it seemingly offered numerous tempting hiding places in its ample wooded areas and secluded corners. Other popular spots for treasure hunters included Tower Grove Park, directly across the street from the apartment on Arsenal Street where Heady had been arrested; the spacious Missouri Botanical Garden directly behind the park; various alleyways behind any of the many South St. Louis taverns Hall and Heady had stopped at soon after their arrival in the city; and assorted farm acreage, cemeteries, and woods as Route 66 continued past the Coral Court motel. In 1953, that highway ran directly through St. Louis, exiting southwestward towards Oklahoma.

Countless others in Kansas City and St. Joseph were scouring riverbeds, woods, and any area remotely within driving or walking distance of any of the places Heady and Hall had been during the course of their crime. The newspapers were also filled with numerous theories about what happened to the money.

One area that held a particular interest for the police was the bank of the Meramec River in South County, after it was learned that Hall had purchased a shovel, garbage cans, and a paper preservative. In his confession, he had revealed that he spent three hours alone in a rented car on the previous Tuesday afternoon. After patiently checking and rechecking the stories told to them by Hall and Hager, police theorized that he may actually have used his purchases to bury the illegal treasure, and that his claim that all of the ransom was still in the hotel room at the time of his arrest was a deception. In support of that theory, Hager reported that when Hall did arrive at the Coral Court three hours after they parted company at Hampton Village in the 5700 block of Chippewa Street, the tyres and fenders of Hall's rented green Plymouth were liberally plastered with fresh mud. That was one of the few things in Hager's statement to the police that was not a lie.

The police also began a door-to-door canvas of the business establishments on the 5700 block of Chippewa, and soon hit pay dirt. Mrs. William Koenig, a clerk at the Hardware Mart at 5755 Chippewa, recalled that a man answering to Hall's description had bought two galvanized iron garbage cans, two large transparent plastic zipper-closing bags, a can of spray-type preservative used for waterproofing paper or fabric, and a shovel. She remembered carrying the man's purchases to his car, but was not able to identify the model. She made two trips, and told police that Hall did not appear to be intoxicated. After the merchandise was placed in the car's rear seat, Hall drove away towards the west.

The Meramec River flowed under a bridge on Route 66 a few miles west of the Coral Court motel. The banks consisted mostly of soft muck, and in many places were bordered by trees and underbrush. Although Hall admitted to FBI agents that he had bought the materials from the hardware store in an effort to bury part of the ransom, he insisted that he mostly drove around the countryside, unable to find a suitable hiding place. Eventually, he told them, he abandoned the project and left the cans and other materials in a deserted clubhouse before driving back to the city to meet Hager. Unconvinced, the FBI made repeated visits to Hall's cell during the day, and at least once took him from his cell to tour the city. Suspecting that Hall was lying when he denied being the one who killed Bobby, they also believed that he was dissembling when he insisted that he had all of the ransom money with him at the time of his arrest. The mere idea that two policemen had brazenly stolen half of the ransom in such a highly publicized case defied not only the usual standards of human decency, but common sense. Moreover, Hall himself had admitted buying materials to be used to hide the money, a clerk had corroborated that story, and Meramec River mud was plastered on the tyres of his rented Plymouth. It just seemed a matter of time before he confessed to the killing, and then to burying half the ransom.

By Saturday, October 10, four days after Hall's and Heady's arrests, both federal and state officials were convinced that Marsh was only a "fall guy," and that Hall and Heady had committed both the kidnapping and murder of Bobby. But they delayed transferring the pair to Kansas City so that they could continue to interrogate Hall about the missing ransom. In Washington, U.S. attorney general Herbert Brownell announced that both prisoners would be turned over to the state of Missouri for prosecution. Both Richard K. Phelps of Jackson County, which encompassed Kansas City; and John E. Downs of Buchanan County, which encompassed St. Joseph, were insisting that they receive the prisoners for trial in their respective jurisdictions, but the evidence suggested that Downs might yield since the strongest case could probably be made on the kidnapping charge in Kansas City. Ultimately, federal authorities were awarded jurisdiction in the case because the kidnappers had crossed state lines.

By now, the FBI had traced Hager's movements after he and Hall had parted ways just before noon on Tuesday, October 6. The bureau was able to confirm that after Hall and Hager reunited at the Villanova Inn, after failing to hook up at the Pink House, they ate sandwiches and drank beer. Ace Cab driver Joseph Travis confirmed that he had driven Hager to the Town House, where the latter allegedly booked a room for Hall and paid $185 in cash for a month's rent. But the bureau was still not able to confirm that Hager, while waiting for his suit to be altered at Boyd's, had called Shoulders, as both men insisted.

The FBI also contacted Patton, asking him to go to the federal building in St. Joseph on October 10. The second letter that Hall wrote to the attorney was the first to arrive—the one he had given to O'Day to mail from California. O'Day, in fact, did mail it, although from Kansas City. The bureau had intercepted it. It also intercepted the first letter Hall wrote to Patton, and the second to arrive. Six cents postage was due on that letter, which caused the delay in delivery. The envelope contained $500 in cash, and in the accompanying letter Hall asked Patton to pay the McCord-Bell auto rental agency for the blue Ford that Heady had rented, and advised the lawyer to keep quiet. "Mrs. Heady has been in a little trouble in Kansas City," the note said, but provided no details.

Patton opened the letters in the presence of four FBI agents, who avoided touching the currency, turning them over only with a pencil.

Meanwhile, police departments around the country continued to look for Thomas John Marsh, the thirty-seven-year-old ex-convict wanted for questioning in the Greenlease case. Police made repeated visits to a small farm near Springfield, Missouri, to talk to Thomas Marsh, Sr. Bearded and disabled, the older Marsh told police that he had not seen his son since they had quarrelled in February and the younger man was ordered to leave. He did add, though, that he did not think his son would ever kill anyone.

On Sunday, October 11, FBI agents scouring the lonely field of wheat stubble where Bobby was killed recovered the brown hat that blew off Heady's head, as well as Bobby's mechanical pencil. Tenant farmer Arthur Brulez had come across the hat the previous day, while on his way to care for several calves, and kicked it aside, not guessing its significance. He came forward only after observing FBI agents, sheriff's deputies, and reporters on the scene, and learned what had happened. Mrs. Mike Olsen, who lived on a neighbouring farm, also found out why her Collie dog had howled night after night, beginning on Monday, September 28. She explained to reporters that so many trucks backfired on the nearby highway that she would not have noticed the sound of a shot being fired. FBI agents also discovered several bloodstains. After spending several hours digging holes, sifting dirt, and closely examining the area along a tall hedgerow, the agents left. Officers were posted to prevent anyone from entering the field.

Finally, around midnight on Monday, October 12, Hall and Heady broke down and made a full confession to Kansas City police chief Bernard Brannon and Joseph E. Thornton, head of the St. Louis FBI office. Starting Saturday night, agents and police working in pairs had questioned the couple about each new piece of evidence obtained—the ballistic tests, the recovery of a bullet from the station wagon, and other details. During this and previous interrogations, an enlarged photograph of Bobby had been placed on a table directly in front of Hall's line of vision. Hall repeatedly tried to avoid looking at it.

As Hall and Heady began to make certain admissions, a call went out for Warden E. E. Hensley, because the agents wanted him to be present when statements were taken. Finally, Brannon said to Hall, "Carl, we don't buy this stuff about the boy being with Marsh. The boy is dead and is buried in the backyard under those flowers at St. Joseph, isn't he? Why don't you tell us all about it?"

Hall gazed at the photograph of Bobby, tears welled in his eyes, and he said to Brannon, "Chief, get me a drink of whisky and I will tell you everything. I've got to have some whisky."

Brannon asked St. Louis chief of police Jeremiah O'Connell for permission to get whisky for Hall. It was still early in the morning. O'Connell replied that getting whisky for Hall would be possible once the bars opened at 6 A.M. "All right, I'll tell the truth," Hall said. After confessing that he had killed Bobby, he sobbed hysterically for ten minutes.

One of three women being held in the city jail with Heady, Bonnie Yonover, told a reporter for the *St. Louis Post-Dispatch* that she had befriended the accused murderess, who allegedly told her that the original kidnapping plan was Hall's, but that she had "put the finishing touches on it." Heady allegedly expressed no remorse, and considerable irritation over Hall's bungling. "If he had stayed with me," she said, alluding to his leaving her at the Arsenal Street apartment and going to the Coral Court, "everything would have been all right." Still under the illusion that she would receive a sentence of only twenty-five years, and with good behaviour might be released in about seven years, a thoroughly unrepentant Heady told Yonover, referring to her share of the ransom: "That $300,000 wouldn't have been too bad for only seven years. I'd rather be dead than poor." She also said, "Before the kidnapping, I thought Carl was a big tough guy with a lot of nerve. But I found out when the chips were down he was nothing but a weakling. He certainly had me fooled."

Two jail matrons, Grace Koenig and Grace Gates, also talked to reporters about their prisoner. "I have never seen a colder, more scheming woman in my life," Gates said. "Right after she was captured and brought here, she was looking at a picture of herself in a newspaper and she remarked, 'That's a terrible picture of me.' I said, 'No, it looks just as you are, Bonnie.'"

Heady had at least one sympathetic observer, a woman who wrote an anonymous letter to *The Kansas City Star* that read in part, "As a divorcée, you are scared, always reminded of your ex-husband or suitor's prosperous business, his happiness with the new bride. You are approached on street corners or by telephone; forsaken by your so-called good friends; left alone to battle the disgrace, humiliation . . . it leads then to drinking, drugs, murder. Divorcées number in the thousands. They need help to keep us in society, in maintaining our standing in life."

Hall and Heady were taken to the Jackson County Court House jail in Kansas City, Missouri, departing under heavy guard from St. Louis around 10 P.M. on Monday, October 12. Federal marshals used a little known exit to spirit the kidnappers away, and also used two private automobiles—one each for Hall and Heady—instead of agency vehicles. The two-car convoy made only one stop, in Columbia. Hall and Heady mostly slept, though Hall did say to Deputy Marshal Leslie S. Davison, "I would like to see those folks [the Greenlease family] get their money back." At another point, he said, "You may not believe this, but I don't know what I did with the missing money." He did recall, though, trying to bury the money; and he also admitted, "If I had listened to her [Heady], I don't think I would have been caught."

Davison later remarked that he did not think Hall was a confirmed drug addict. "He is clear and speaks well," the deputy marshal said, "and is neither surly nor sarcastic, as many prisoners are."

After a five-and-a-half-hour drive, the group arrived at the jail at 3:35 on Tuesday morning. Fearing a lynch mob, the authorities had refused to release any information about when the prisoners would leave from St. Louis, or even whether the U.S. attorney in Kansas City had issued orders to transfer the prisoners.

Hall's anger momentarily flared after the long drive when weary deputy marshals shoved him somewhat roughly against the rear wall of an elevator in the courthouse to make room for other guards. Just as quickly, though, he assumed the sullen indifference he had wrapped himself in. Heady, who had not had an opportunity to talk to him since they left St. Louis, crowded close to him and tried to cheer him up.

"Honey, are you tired?" she asked. But he ignored her. Already, whatever anger and resentment she may have harboured against her lover and co-conspirator had all but evaporated. The pair were then put into separate cells on the eleventh floor of the courthouse. Also being held in the same jail as a material witness was Sandra O'Day.

After Hall and Heady rested, FBI agents began questioning both of them separately early that afternoon, using lie detectors and recording their answers with a tape recorder. When they were returned to their respective cells, both had to spend the night in complete darkness. Sheriff Arvid Owsley explained that all electric current to the cell block had been cut off because of exposed wiring, which either prisoner, or both, could use to commit suicide. For the same reason, he said, running water was also cut off, and guards were stationed outside both cells around the clock. Sentiment among the prison population towards the kidnappers, he said, was "vicious."

Edward L. Scheufler, the U.S. attorney in Kansas City, announced that plans were proceeding to convene a federal grand jury. The fifty-four-year-old Scheufler, a former city councilman who had made a name for himself opposing corrupt political boss Tom Pendergast, had successfully prosecuted three out of the six kidnappers sentenced to death under the Lindbergh Law in the federal court system.

He explained that his decision to try the prisoners on federal kidnapping charges instead of state charges was based on a desire to get a verdict rendered as quickly as possible. In a state court, both defendants would have to be tried separately; but in federal court, they could be tried together. Also, in a federal court there would be no doubt about the admissibility as evidence of money recovered from Hall, while in state court there might be. He added that, if Hall and Heady somehow escaped conviction on federal charges, they would still face kidnapping charges in Jackson County and first-degree murder charges in Kansas, both of which carried the death penalty.

In subsequent days, guards reported hearing both Heady and Hall weeping in their cells.

7.

A Tale of Two Cities

In succeeding weeks, prosecutors in Kansas City continued to build their case against Hall and Heady, while in St. Louis investigators were increasingly turning their attention to Shoulders's whereabouts on the afternoon and evening of Hall's arrest. The twofold ongoing drama in the westernmost and easternmost parts of the state, one on the banks of the Missouri River and the other on the Mississippi's, ultimately came down to seeking answers to two questions: How soon would the kidnappers be put to death? Where was the missing ransom money?

Public opinion and prosecutors were virtually united in harbouring no doubt about the answer to the first question. Bobby Greenlease's abductors were guilty of kidnapping and murder, and would be executed in the Missouri gas chamber—sooner rather than later. (Two lone doubters were Hall, who at first worried whether he would be electrocuted in Kansas's state prison in Leavenworth, or gassed in the Missouri State Penitentiary in Jefferson City; and Heady, who was still hopeful of a twenty-five-year sentence with parole after seven years.)

But the certitude in Kansas City was offset in St. Louis by bafflement, doubt, false leads, lies, duplicity, and dead ends, as investigators made little headway in their search for the missing half of the ransom.

The sentiments of a shocked nation were summarized by *Time* magazine, which noted, in reporting on the arrest of the kidnappers: "Hall disclosed the most grisly details of the whole horrifying crime, one of the worst in U.S. history."

The headline of a front-page story in the *St. Louis Post-Dispatch* read: "State Officials Pressing Hunt for Marsh in Kidnapping Case," even though the police were no longer seeking him as a suspect. Rather, they considered it significant that he had not come forward during the investigation, and simply wanted to talk to him.

In a much publicized interview with the *St. Louis Globe-Democrat*, Shoulders claimed that Hall told him, on the night of his arrest, that he planned to kill Heady with the same gun he used to kill Bobby. Dismissing her as "nothing but a drunken bum," Hall allegedly told the detective that she was the only person who could have been identified—thus the need to eliminate her. Shoulders also declared that, when he was arrested, Hall had said to him, "Look, officer, you just know me as Byrne. Suppose you take one of those suitcases of money, and I'll take the other, and walk out of here as Byrne." Of course, said Shoulders, he had righteously rejected the offer.

Hall's admission that he planned to kill Heady, and his offer of a bribe, were not entirely implausible. But on the face of it they were unlikely. Shoulders may have concocted these tales because he wanted only to throw investigators—and the press—off his scent. Whatever Hall's true feelings toward Heady prior to the kidnapping, he had ample opportunity to kill her once he had the ransom—at the very moment he picked up the duffel bag containing the money when it was thrown off the wooden bridge, for example. Or even before he picked up the ransom. But Hall also knew that, once she was reported missing, or her body was found and identified, Heady's neighbours—not to mention countless Kansas City bartenders—would certainly have been able to identify Hall as her lover. Moreover, on the night of his arrest, Hall had stubbornly denied killing Bobby, absolved Heady of blame, and confessed to the crime only six days later.

Sandra O'Day told investigators, as she had from the very beginning, that she and Hall did not have sex at the Coral Court. She was contradicted by Hager, who said that O'Day told him the two did have sex. Hall also insisted that he did not have sex with the prostitute, saying that both of them merely lay side by side on the bed. Both were so drunk, he claimed, that he did not even make a pass. Possibly, both Hager and Hall were telling the truth as they saw it. The cabdriver was, after all, O'Day's pimp, and perhaps O'Day had only wanted to assure him during their ride together, after leaving the motel, that she had earned her money.

Once they settled into their cells at the Jackson County jail, Hall lapsed into sullen silence. Heady asked for a pencil so that she could work on a crossword puzzle, but her request was denied because she was classified as a "maximum security prisoner." Instead she was given a comic book, *Intimate Love*, to read.

On October 19, the St. Louis Board of Police Commissioners launched a formal inquiry into the missing ransom money. Chief O'Connell told reporters that he doubted the entire amount had ever been brought to St. Louis. Astonishingly, the FBI had refused to provide the police department with copies of Hall's and Heady's full confessions, and O'Connell was unaware of Hall's insistence that he had both suitcases in his possession when he was arrested. But police investigators did want to know why Shoulders had left the station house shortly after booking Hall. Mudd's call had gone out at 9:32 P.M., soon after Hall was booked at 8:57 P.M., so where was Shoulders?

At first, O'Connell simply accepted as true the version concocted by Shoulders and Dolan about how they had brought two half-full suitcases into the station house when Hall was arrested. "It is hard for me to believe that any policeman would take that much money," he told reporters. "I can see, if he had any larceny in his soul, he might pick up a package of $10 or $20 bills—but not $300,000."

On the morning of October 19, Dolan gave a statement. The commissioners then went to the Town House to take photographs, measurements, and notes, and to examine the premises. That afternoon, Jean Fletcher, the manager of the Town House, testified. Dolan was then re-interviewed in Fletcher's presence. Hager testified on the second day. All three witnesses kept to their original stories.

The police had originally announced that the board of inquiry would not question Shoulders, although he was credited with solving the case, because he was suffering from a nervous condition brought on by the investigation and subsequent inexplicable disappearance of the ransom. The detective's physician explained that Shoulders needed rest, and that interviewing him might adversely affect his health. No doubt also adversely affecting Shoulders's health was a blunt warning from Costello not to implicate him in the disappearance of the ransom.

Shoulders then abruptly changed his mind and, on the third day of the inquiry, agreed to testify. Asked about his whereabouts after booking Hall, he said he had driven his private car to his home to allow his landlady, June Marie George, to use it, because he expected the interrogation of Hall to last through the night. In his official report, he had made no mention of his absence from the station. He clashed bitterly with commissioner Herman Willer about a stakeout he claimed to be on, on the afternoon of Hall's arrest. Shoulders refused to give information about the stakeout, saying that information was confidential. Other ranking officers said they had no knowledge of any such surveillance.

A few days later, on October 25, Shoulders angrily resigned from the force, saying that the police inquiry has ruined his reputation. In his letter of resignation he said, "After twenty-seven years as a police officer, to be castigated and have my character assassinated, on the heels of performing my duty with the highest sense of responsibility, is more than I can endure with any degree of self-respect and pride."

For the first time, Shoulders also claimed that he had received a second tip that would have led him to the Greenlease kidnappers even if Hager had not telephoned him. But he emphatically refused to divulge the name of the informant. "I've never told anybody who it is. I haven't told the FBI, and I never will tell anybody," he said. Then he added, "It'll be found out," without explaining how.

The police department, however, refused to accept his resignation. That same day, the police arrested Hager, searched the house where his estranged wife lived, and questioned him for eight hours. The police revealed that they were acting on a tip that the missing money was buried in the Hagers' basement. Shoulders suggested to reporters that, in his opinion, a group of local hoodlums—whom he did not identify—had gotten hold of the missing ransom. He discounted a theory that some of the ransom had been mailed to St. Joseph from an East St. Louis post office. A man had been reported mailing a heavy package to St. Joseph from that post office some days earlier. Police investigators had learned that Hall asked for a cardboard box when he purchased a radio soon after moving into his Arsenal Street apartment, and was pleased when the clerk presented him with a large one. The possibility that he had used the box to mail some of the ransom was just one of many false leads they were pursuing.

Hampering the police department's investigation was the inexplicable refusal of the FBI to cooperate. Asked what kind of cooperation the department had received from the federal agency, Chief O'Connell bluntly replied: "Absolutely none." He complained that FBI agents would not even tell him whether O'Day had been arrested.

On October 27, a U.S. grand jury in Kansas City began hearing evidence seeking an indictment against Hall and Heady. Robert C.

Greenlease was the first witness. In all, about twenty-five witnesses were called to testify. The previous day, Shoulders had declared that he would refuse to testify on grounds that it would incriminate him; his resignation from the police force still had not been accepted. The next day, having changed his mind, he testified for three hours.

Shoulders had steadfastly refused to identify his second tipster, saying he would rather go to prison or die than do so. But in a secret session of the grand jury, he did admit that it was Costello, while continuing to maintain the fiction that Hager was his first tipster. "I was trying to find out [what happened to the money] and he [Costello] was trying to use the same sources," Shoulders testified. "I have confidence in him and I think he was trying to find out about the money, but he could have misinformed me. I don't want to make a forecast—he might be in on the deal. . . . I think if he had been in on a deal like this at first and then was informed by me what it was [a kidnapping], he would have backed away from it." Shoulders told the grand jury that he no longer hoped to find the missing money and thought it had probably been burned.

Asked why he thought Costello had contacted him and not another officer, Shoulders replied, "I think he picked me because he drove a cab with me and had known me for a long time. I want to keep his name out. I don't like to say this braggingly. He is an ex-convict and an associate of thieves and belongs to the underworld. He told me I was the only man he would deal with, and if I give my word I would live up to it."

Asked if he suspected that his second tipster stole the money, Shoulders said, "I suspected he knew who stole it. I always suspected."

When the *St. Louis Post-Dispatch* obtained a transcript of Shoulders's testimony and revealed that Shoulders had identified Costello as the second informant, the mobster phoned the detective and insisted that he change his story and say it was someone else.

Depressed, frightened, and altogether miserable, Shoulders complied, and told reporters that his second tipster was, in fact, not Costello but someone else.

Still in handcuffs, O'Day also testified, though she provided no new information to the grand jury. Reporters and photographers rushed into the corridor on hearing she would be brought from the Jackson County jail. In the courthouse, O'Day was identified as the former Mary Ann Melvin of Du Quoin, Illinois, and the former wife of Raymond Day.

Meanwhile, the mystery of Thomas Marsh remained unsolved. His father told reporters that he was convinced his son had been murdered. The older Marsh's daughter, Rose Marie, informed the FBI that she was not even aware that she had a brother until the bureau began its investigation.

On November 1, less than a month after arresting Hall, and just a week after he resigned from the police department in anger at the Board of Police Commissioners, Shoulders and June Marie George flew to the island of Maui in Hawaii. Although they travelled under the assumed names of Sherman Woodlaw and Mrs. Mae H. Rossi, they were immediately recognized at the Honolulu airport. Shoulders told reporters, "I'm not Lieutenant Shoulders. I'm ex-Lieutenant Shoulders."

Shoulders also said that he was "sick and tired" and "just fed up with talking about" the Greenlease case. Moreover, he was convinced that the missing $300,000 would be found, and emphasized that he would not have been so foolish as to steal it because it had "a red lantern on it." On previous occasions, he had theorized that the ransom had been stolen by "hoodlums," or had been burned.

"I got the kidnapper," he said. "I got the gun. I didn't get the money, but they'll find it."

On that same day, police and federal agents revealed they had established that Hall's two suitcases were not brought into the Newstead station at the time of his arrest. The finding was considered a breakthrough, and was based on the testimony of several witnesses at the station at the time.

The trial of Hall and Heady began on the morning of Monday, November 16, fifty days after Bobby was killed, in federal court in Kansas City, with seventy-nine-year-old Judge Albert L. Reeves presiding.

That morning, just before proceedings began, Heady wrote to Clinton L. Allen, a monument dealer in Maryville, Missouri, whom her former husband had known for many years. Heady asked Allen to select a tombstone for her because "I might be needing it." She also asked him to care for Doc, her registered boxer, describing it as a prizewinner at many shows, while also cautioning that it was a "meanie." Allen maintained a dog kennel in addition to his monument business. She told Allen that she wanted to be buried at Clearmont, in Nodaway County, where she had been born forty-one years earlier.

In contrast to Heady's quiet demeanour in her prison cell, said reporter Bill Moore of *The Kansas City Star*, "she is jaunty as she enters the courtroom. Her eyes sweep across the press tables, and she swivels her chair and glances back to the spectators. There is defiance in that glance. But it is plain that if there was someone— just one person—in the courtroom to smile and nod at her that she would be pleased to return the smile." But there was no one to smile back at.

The trial lasted only three days, and the jury found both Hall and Heady guilty within eight minutes of convening in the jury room. Throughout the trial, every seat in the large, walnut-lined courtroom was filled, and many more spectators waited in the corridor.

The trial opened with the bailiff intoning, "God save the United States and this honourable court," causing Heady to put her hand over her mouth to stifle a giggle.

In his opening statement, U.S. Attorney Scheufler described

the kidnapping and murder of Bobby Greenlease as "one of the outstanding kidnappings in the annals of America—in the entire world." He also told the jury that, just days before the kidnapping, Hall and Heady decided that it would be necessary to kill the boy—though, of course, Hall had made that decision months beforehand, as his elaborate preparations for Bobby's burial proved.

Hall's court-appointed defence lawyer was Roy K. Dietrich, president of the Kansas City Bar Association, who had entered a guilty plea on Hall's behalf—not to kidnapping, but to murder, in a gambit to avoid the death penalty for his client. In his opening statement, Dietrich admitted that neither he nor his client disputed any of the charges that Scheufler had just recounted. But, he added, Hall "was used to wild and riotous living. He did not know how to work. He tasted the joys of money, without knowing what it was to toil for it. He did not have the love from his parents that a child should have."

Harold Hull of Maryville, Missouri, assumed the role of Heady's defence attorney after William Rosenthal of St. Joseph, her original lawyer, withdrew from the case, without giving any reason, after spending an hour conversing with her in the Jackson County jail. Hull had represented Heady during her divorce and in other matters, and now also arranged for her to transfer ownership of her house to her aunt Nellie, who as a young woman used to drive Bonnie to basketball games. Nellie's married name was Baker, and she was to be Heady's only family support in the months ahead.

Like Dietrich, Hull entered a plea of guilty to a charge of murder on his client's behalf, in a similar hope that she might escape the death penalty.

Scheufler then spent forty-five minutes reading Heady's twenty-six-page typewritten confession into the court record. Heady sat quietly at the defence table, staring at the floor. Only once did she show any emotion—when Scheufler read: "I wanted to stay drunk so that my conscience wouldn't bother me."

During the trial, Hall sat diagonally across from Heady, looking hopeless and depressed. FBI agent Arthur S. Reeder read Hall's thirty-six-page confession. While it was being entered into the court record, Hall kept his hand on his chin. His eyes were downcast, and he blinked frequently.

Bobby's father, sitting with his friends Robert Ledterman and Norbert O'Neill in the back of the courtroom, swallowed hard and worked his jaw when the confession recounted the actual killing of Bobby. Hall bit his knuckles. Several spectators sobbed openly. Both the St. Louis Police Department and the public were startled by one new piece of information—Hall's insistence that neither of the two pieces of luggage containing the eighty-five pounds of $10 and $20 bills was taken to the police station when he was booked. "At the time of my arrest," Hall declared in his confession, "I had been drinking, but definitely was not drunk or under the influence of narcotics, and was aware of the incidents which transpired during my arrest."

In describing his arrest by Shoulders and Dolan, he noted that he and Dolan walked the length of the hotel corridor, looking for a rear stairway, while Shoulders stayed behind. "We were unable to locate any steps there," Hall said, "and as we turned to go back, looking up the hallway, I noticed a man standing at the end of the hallway facing my room. I am not positive but this man appeared to be talking to someone in the direction of my room, but I was not able to hear any of the conversation."

That man in the hallway, of course, was Costello, and the person in the hotel room to whom he was talking was Hager.

Defence attorney Hull informed the court that Heady desired no one to testify on her behalf. Nevertheless, he did intend to call one witness for his client—Nellie Baker, Heady's aunt, who had raised her. Heady painted her fingernails red and was wearing a two-piece black suit and brightly coloured earrings that Baker had bought for her to wear. She had also brought other suits, dresses, hats, and jewellery for her niece to wear on subsequent days of the trial. Hall, always the flashy dresser as a young man, wore a brown gabardine suit throughout the trial that had cost him $55.75.

Among the early witnesses was Soeur Morand, who sat with her crucifix on her lap. Asked to identify the woman who had taken Bobby from the French Institute on the morning of September 28, the nun hesitated, briefly scanned the courtroom, and pointed at Heady, who stared back impassively at her accuser. Hall looked down at his shoes.

Bobby's father also took the stand, and was able to speak only with great effort. He was given the government's exhibit number 4, a mechanical pencil, and identified it as Bobby's. Returning to the rear of the courtroom, he stared hard at Hall and Heady. Tears welled in his eyes, but he said nothing as he struggled to maintain his composure.

Dolan, in his sworn testimony, denied ever taking the walk down the hotel corridor described by Hall, and also said that he never saw a stranger such as the one Hall described. He remained adamant that he and Shoulders had brought the two suitcases with them when they brought Hall to the Newstead station for booking. In an exchange with Dietrich, the policeman also denied taking any keys from Hall at the time of his arrest.

Q. Who went into the closet? After the FBI have told us and after about fifteen days of working on it, and he [Hall] said that the suitcase clicked, who was that did that? Was that you or Shoulders that went into the clothes closet where those suitcases were?

A. Lieutenant Shoulders went in the clothes closet.

Q. Did you hear the suitcases click?

A. No, sir.

Q. Did you see him take the keys in there?

A. No, sir.

Q. Do you know anything about the keys at all?

A. Not that I recall there.

Q. After the FBI had worked on this matter from the seventh of October until the twenty-fourth of October and had pretty well gotten the facts and they prepared a statement here—you have read it, haven't you?

A. Yes, sir; yes, sir, I did.

Q. As far as you know that is pretty accurate, isn't it?

A. I guess the statement is accurate.

Q. You think it is? You have read it, haven't you?

A. Yes, sir.

Q. You want to state to this jury that you think that statement is accurate?

A. In part, yes, sir.

Q. And what wasn't accurate?

A. He said positively none of the baggage went to the police station. That is inaccurate.

Throughout the day's testimony, *Time* reported, Heady appeared to show no remorse. "She lolled, squinted and smiled, scratched her nose, plucked at her shoulder straps."

During the second day of the trial, Bobby's mother was called to testify. Appearing fairly composed, and wearing a grey flannel suit, she slipped through the rear door of the courtroom and took the witness stand. Heady glanced up at her only once, and then looked away. Hall, his elbow propped on the defence table and supporting his jaw with a cupped hand, did not look up at all.

"I talked with [Hall] four times on the telephone," Virginia Greenlease said. "I told him we were willing and ready to pay the money. I asked always about Bobby. . . . I asked, When will we have Bobby?"

Her eyes remained dry as she testified, and her voice never faltered as she answered the questions Scheufler put to her, but at times she was almost inaudible. Some spectators gasped when she recounted how Hall assured her that Bobby was alive.

A table next to the witness stand contained the prosecution's exhibits, including the shovel Hall used to dig Bobby's grave. Also on the table were Hall's Smith & Wesson, the bag containing the lime used to cover Bobby's body, and the hat that Heady lost when her dog leaped and strained at the leash when Bobby was shot.

When Virginia Greenlease finished testifying, Scheufler turned to the defence counsel and inquired matter-of-factly, "Any questions?"

Appearing startled, Hull quickly answered, "No, no."

Dietrich, his voice trembling, added, "Of course not. I'm just sorry she had to come."

Hall, seemingly unnerved by Virginia Greenlease's appearance, whispered to a deputy marshal that he wanted a recess. Judge Reeves granted a five-minute recess, and Hall, flanked by guards, left the room. Heady, brightening, leaned over to talk to Hull. Robert Greenlease remained at his customary post in the rear of the courtroom with his loyal friends, Ledterman and O'Neill.

Others appearing on behalf of the prosecution during the trial included radio repairman Frank Maulding, who installed the shortwave converter in Hall's car; the salesman at Sam's Loan who sold Hall the Smith & Wesson; Grace Hatfield, who sold Hall a shovel at her hardware store; and the manager of the Sawyer Material Company who sold Hall a sack of lime.

Mrs. Garnett Travis, who knew the Hall family, testified for the defence that Hall's father was a very stern man and that she had never seen any physical display of affection between father and son. Speaking of Zella Hall, Carl's mother, Mrs. Travis said, "I think she loved him like any mother loves a child," but she added that Zella "seemed afraid that the younger generation was not very good, and it was hard to get them to do anything."

Another defence witness was Zella Hall's old friend, Samuel Tucker, now eighty years old, who had hired Hall to work at the Pleasanton telephone company with his mother's connivance to keep the young boy off the streets. Hall had been "a carefree boy with a smile on his face" when he signed up with the Marines,

Tucker told the court. But after he returned from fighting in Okinawa and other theatres of war, Tucker related, Hall had turned into "a person who was cold and hard. He was not as warm, not as friendly."

Though Heady seemed almost disinterested in the proceedings when her own confession had been read the previous day, she was clearly wounded by Hall's frequent references in his confession to her near-constant drunken stupor, beginning with the murder of Bobby until her arrest. The only time she showed genuine emotion, though, occurred when Pansy McDowall of La Cygne, Kansas, appeared on the witness stand. McDowall had taken young Carl into her house for a short time after the death of his father and Zella Hall had found herself unable to control the troubled young boy.

"Carl was one of the most grateful and appreciative children I have ever seen in my life," McDowall said. "He was elaborately formal, elaborately polite and courteous." As she related young Hall's sorrow over the death of his father, and his wish that he could be with his Tomama, Heady's eyes glistened with tears and she used a handkerchief to wipe them away. When she glanced across the counsel table at Hall, she saw that his cheeks were flushed and that he seemed to be fighting back tears. He did not return her gaze.

"Now just what kind of a mother was Carl Hall's mother?" Dietrich asked.

"She was busy—always busy with her club work and with social affairs," Mrs. McDowall answered. "She was a fine woman, and she was intelligent and a woman with a good business head. But as a mother she was the most cold-blooded and hardest-hearted mother I have ever known."

During the trial, Hall resented the testimony by McDowall and other Pleasanton townsfolk that suggested his mother might be partly responsible for his going bad because she was so involved in social affairs.

"No one could have a finer mother than I had," he told the Reverend George L. Evans of St. Paul's Episcopal Church in Kansas City, Kansas, who had gone to the prison to counsel him, "and the same goes for my father. I had wonderful parents. Their actions were in no way responsible for my going bad."

Hall's almost childlike devotion to his mother—who had, after all, disinherited him—was in stark contrast to his heartless indifference to Virginia Greenlease's almost unimaginable suffering after Bobby was abducted. If he was aware of the irony, he never spoke about it.

In his closing arguments, Hull pointed out that Nellie Baker testified that Heady had lived a normal life for forty years. Drinking had been her downfall. After all, he noted, she had plenty of money and "was probably worth $50,000 or $60,000 and a farm, a home, an automobile" at the time of the kidnapping. Unfortunately, he added, she was "putty" in Hall's hands. He had planned the kidnapping, bought the shovel, dug the grave, and killed Bobby. Certainly, said Hull, she deserved to be punished. But would taking her life benefit society in any way? "If I thought so," he said, "I would not oppose it." He left it to the consciences of the jurors to decide her fate, but declared that he was opposed to the death penalty, and that only a Supreme Being "could determine an adequate punishment for a person who has sinned."

Dietrich, in his closing arguments, concurred with Hull that "It would be a popular act to give this man death. The newspapers have tried him, they have condemned him to death; the radio has condemned him to death. There is a clamour throughout the world as to this man." He revealed that, in a conference with Hall the previous week, the defendant had declared his remorse, and told him, "I am ready to go to the gas chamber." Noting that the prosecutor had brought in "too many witnesses," he added that Mr. and Mrs. Greenlease should have been spared the ordeal of testifying.

Dietrich also reviewed Hall's childhood—how he had been without a father from the age of twelve; that his mother had been a very busy woman; that he never learned the value of money. He reviewed the testimony of Samuel Tucker, the loyal family friend, who suggested that war had changed Hall from an upstanding citizen. "I don't know what war does to a man," Dietrich said. "Except here is a man, a fine citizen, who knew him, a man eighty years old. You saw Sam Tucker, and Sam tells you Hall came back hard, cynical, not the boy that he was before he went into the Marines." He concluded by saying it was up to the jury to decide whether Hall deserved the death penalty or life imprisonment.

Scheufler's rebuttal was to the point: "What ye sow, so shall ye reap," he told the jurors, quoting the biblical injunction. Both Hall and Heady, he declared, had come from better than average homes, and that made their crime even more horrible because they had more of an opportunity than most people to make something of themselves.

Judge Reeves gave brief instructions to the jurors, and at 10:44 they retired to deliberate. In less than an hour, at 11:42, they solemnly returned. Since the defendants had entered guilty pleas, the only question was whether the jury would recommend a death sentence or life imprisonment. Few spectators were surprised at how quickly a verdict had been reached, and even fewer—if any—doubted what that verdict would be. Hall and Heady sat quietly. Reeves asked if a verdict had been reached, and the foreman rose, saying, "Yes, sir." He handed a piece of paper to the clerk, who passed it to the judge. The judge had given the jury a sheet of paper in advance of deliberations. It asked:

"Do you recommend that the death penalty be imposed?"

The foreman simply had to write in the word "yes" or "no."

"Yes" was written in twice, once for Hall and once for Heady.

When the clerk read out the verdict, several people in the courtroom applauded. Some even whistled. The bailiff pounded his gavel, demanding order. Each juror was polled. Reeves called both defendants before the bench, and they quietly approached, accompanied by their attorneys. Heady had smiled wanly on hearing the verdict; Hall appeared glum.

"Do either of you have any statement why you should not be put to death?" Reeves asked.

"No, sir," Hall responded, loudly and clearly.

Heady shook her head and said, simply, "Nothing."

Reeves ruled that Carl Austin Hall and Bonnie Brown Heady were to die in the gas chamber at the Missouri State Penitentiary in Jefferson City, Missouri, on December 18, 1953. Both Hall and Heady accepted the judge's sentence stoically. They had long since resigned themselves to their fates, and neither shared their respective attorney's hopes for a life sentence. As the jury's verdict was given, Heady had even glanced quickly across the defence table and smiled defiantly at Hall.

After the sentencing, deputy marshals escorted the condemned pair from the fourth-floor courtroom to the fifth-floor marshal's office until the crowd of spectators dispersed. Both seemed almost nonchalant during the trip from the courthouse back to the Jackson County jail.

Asked to comment on the sentence, Bobby's father said only, "It's too good for them, but it's the best the law provides."

One of the jurors, it was later learned, had proposed life imprisonment for Heady. After further deliberation, the twelve jurors reached unanimous agreement that both prisoners should be executed. More than five hundred people applied for permission to witness the executions, though the room for spectators in the gas chamber could accommodate only fifty people, and at least thirty of those had to be official witnesses, attending physicians, and prison personnel. Anticipating the death sentences, Colonel Thomas E. Whitecotton, the state director of corrections, announced that the executions would be simultaneous, and revealed that he had written to Warden Harley O. Teets of San Quentin for advice on what Heady—the first woman to be executed at the Missouri State Penitentiary—should wear. Teets replied that Heady ought to be allowed to wear a dress instead of a bathing suit, as was done in the execution of two women in the San Quentin gas chamber. Gas chamber occupants were routinely given as little clothing as possible to wear—usually just shorts—to prevent gas from accumulating in the clothing. The thirty men who had been executed in the Missouri chamber had worn only black shorts, socks, and a black blindfold, and Whitecotton decided on the same garb for Hall.

Bonnie Brown Heady would not be the first woman executed by the federal government. Mary Surratt had been hanged on July 7, 1863, for conspiring in the assassination of Abraham Lincoln. The execution came only eighty-three days after the president's death. Earlier in 1953, a trial even more sensational than that of Hall and Heady had culminated on June 19, 1953, when the kidnappers were still in the planning stage of their plot to abduct Bobby Greenlease. On that day, Julius and Ethel Rosenberg—who were near-contemporaries of Hall and Heady— were electrocuted at Sing Sing Correctional Facility in Ossining, New York, after being convicted of atomic espionage.

Hall and Heady were to be executed in the Missouri State Penitentiary because of an agreement between the state and the federal government. The federal prison system had no means of imposing capital punishment.

Just hours after Hall and Heady had been condemned to death, Hall received a visitor—an old childhood friend from Pleasanton. Mr. Dan Evans had attended the same grade school as Hall, though they were never close and had not seen each other after Hall went off to Kemper Military School. Mr. Evans, whose mother still lived in the small Kansas town where he had grown up, had taken a radically different path from Hall, graduating from the College of Emporia in Emporia, Kansas, and studying theology at a Chicago seminary before being ordained a Presbyterian minister. Currently, he was serving as minister at a church in Topeka, and he had come to see Hall at the request of Marshall Hoag and Dietrich.

The two men met for an hour, from 11 A.M. until noon, in Hall's cell.

"He was grateful that someone from his hometown had come to talk with him," Evans said of Hall, who indicated that he was resigned to being put to death. "He expressed the idea to me that he had committed something horrible, so that he should rightfully be punished by society for having done such a deed."

Hall also wondered why, although they had grown up in the same town, one had chosen to serve God while the other pursued a life that led to the murder of an innocent child.

"He was inclined to place the blame on liquor for what he had done," the minister said. "He said he started drinking and never seemed to be able to stop. He said he started taking drugs in addition to the liquor and that didn't help."

Evans also observed that Hall's parents had been emotionally distant and seldom displayed any outward signs of love and affection towards their only child.

"It brought home to me," Evans said, "that the time parents spend with their children should not be spared, and that many of them need to spend more time with their children."

The two men talked in detail about the kidnapping, though Evans noted that, "as a minister, I don't think I should say too much about what he told me during that time." Evans did note rather dryly, however, that "I am not sure whether he felt particularly remorseful about the whole thing." Although they discussed religious matters, Hall's visitor conceded that "I could not say he expressed the idea that he expected to get any solace out of religion."

During the meeting, Hall revealed that he wished to marry Heady. Just as the hour allotted for the visit was nearly over, the minister persuaded Hall to pray with him for forgiveness. But before the prayer could be completed, the jailer interrupted to say that time was up.

The prayer session had been abruptly terminated because Hall and Heady had a noon date with Judge Reeves. Both prisoners were taken from their cells to stand before the magistrate, who heard from Dietrich that his client did not intend to appeal his sentence. In an earlier conversation with Hull, Reeves had also been informed that Heady did not plan to appeal, either.

Reeves then signed the commitment papers authorizing Acting U.S. Marshal William Tatman to carry out the court's sentence.

"There will be no appeal in this case," he announced. "The matter is all over so far as that's concerned. There will be no foreseeable delay in the execution. The defendants want no appeal."

He also praised Dietrich for representing Hall without compensation, adding, "I wanted a man of unquestioned integrity and of highest legal ability and standing in his profession to act in the case." He further explained that he had asked Dietrich to serve so that "all the world might know that this confessed murderer and kidnapper would have a fair trial before me and that every point would be raised to preserve the rights of the accused."

Dietrich later confirmed that Hall and Heady had asked permission to be married before their execution, while also noting that the Justice Department immediately denied the request. Hall had broached the matter both before and during the trial. "I promised Bonnie," Dietrich quoted Hall as saying to him, "that we were to be married and she wants to. I want to go ahead with it."

After their appearance before Reeves, Hall and Heady were returned to their cells on the eleventh floor of the Jackson County Jail, still handcuffed to waist chains and guarded by marshals. As they shuffled down the corridor, almost side by side, Hall turned around and said something. Both smiled. Then they were put into their respective cells, and their chains were removed.

A few minutes later, they asked for their midday meal. That morning they had skipped breakfast, except for coffee. Seemingly without a care in the world, they devoured a simple lunch of beef stew, bread and butter, and coffee.

Not long afterwards, Father George Evans visited Hall for the third time. Father Evans, who was not related to and was unacquainted with Dan Evans, went to see Hall at the condemned man's invitation. He had known Hall as a student at Kemper Military School, when he was an instructor there before entering the ministry. Father Evans's first visit had been at Dietrich's request. After their conference, the priest told reporters, "When I saw him previous to the trial on two occasions, his first statements were those of remorse. I saw him again this afternoon and, at his request, I talked to Mrs. Heady. This was the first time I had seen Mrs. Heady. She likewise expressed great contrition." As tears welled in his eyes, he added, "There are varied and many problems that come to a parish priest."

8.

Death Row

Moving quickly after the sentencing of Hall and Heady, Marshal Tatman, accompanied by deputy marshals and his wife, who was serving as matron in charge of Heady, arranged to transfer the condemned pair immediately to the Missouri State Penitentiary in Jefferson City, the state capital located between Kansas City and St. Louis. Their execution had been set for "as soon as possible after 12:01 A.M. on December 18," a Friday, Tatman told reporters. Exactly one month earlier, at 2:10 P.M., Friday, November 20, the Tatmans and Hall and Heady, accompanied by deputy marshals, left the Jackson County Jail for the three-hour drive across the state's midsection.

Built on a promontory overlooking the Missouri River, the penitentiary consisted of six red-brick cell blocks, nine factories, and assorted other buildings, all enclosed by turreted limestone walls. The original building, dating to 1839, had been the mansion of James L. Minor, the Missouri secretary of state, and had subsequently been remodelled and extensively expanded.

Upon their arrival at the penitentiary, Heady exchanged her

fashionable black dress, black short coat, and hat for a pale green cotton prison dress.

"It fits better than what I had in Kansas City," she said brightly.

Hall took off the brown gabardine suit he had worn during the three-day trial, and was given beltless khaki trousers and a matching shirt.

"This is a repeat performance for you," Heady quipped, glancing at Hall. While they were being fingerprinted, she cheerfully took up the refrain again, saying, "This is just like a homecoming." Earlier that year, on a Friday in April, Hall had been released after serving fifteen months of a five-year sentence for robbing taxi drivers in Kansas City.

As she crossed the prison yard en route to death row, however, Heady's mood took a more serious turn.

"Some people looked at me so horrible," she said to Bertha Carroll, superintendent of the women's division of the prison, who was escorting her. Heady was shivering from the cold, and Carroll put a coat over the prisoner's shoulders. Heady also told Carroll that the death sentence was exactly what she had hoped for, adding, "I don't think I could have stood a life term."

Prison officials were taking extra security measures, refusing to permit Heady any further use of a manicure set that her aunt Nellie Baker had also given her. But Hall was to be allowed to shave himself each morning with a safety razor as a guard looked on. Word on the prison grapevine was that the kidnappers could expect no sympathy from their fellow prisoners. "Hall was like a sucker who walks in on a fixed gambling game," one prisoner was reported as saying, "and hopes to win the pot. He didn't have a chance. He's just a punk."

The three daily meals for Hall and Heady were to be obtained from the officers' mess, rather than from the convict-manned kitchen, to ensure that neither was poisoned. Other precautions were also taken. Prisoners were known to scorn kidnappers and others who abused or murdered children, and such inmates were often the object of retribution. Many of the prisoners in the Missouri penitentiary also harboured a particular resentment against Hall because they felt that his early release from prison the previous April, followed so quickly by his crime, jeopardized their own chances for parole. Around-the-clock guards were posted outside both Hall's and Heady's cells to prevent a suicide attempt.

"I can't think of anything more embarrassing," said Director of Corrections Whitecotton, "than not having them here on December 18."

From his cell, number 25, Hall could see the gas chamber, a small building across the prison yard. Heady's cell, number 18, looked out upon a solitary sycamore tree. A fine steel mesh was placed over the bars of both Hall's and Heady's cells to prevent anything from being passed into or out of either one.

In anticipation of Heady's arrival, an enclosed shower was installed in death row to allow her some privacy while bathing. Male prisoners bathed in a communal shower, though Hall would bathe alone. Each cell contained a toilet and small washbowl extending from the wall, and a flat, metal-spring cot. The large overhead lights were kept on day and night.

Several cells just below death row were known as "The Hole." Recalcitrant convicts were kept there in solitary confinement, with a board for a bed, and bread and water for rations.

Until Hall and Heady arrived at the Missouri State Penitentiary, death row held only one occupant—a twenty-one-year-old ex-convict named Samuel Norbert Reese, who was awaiting the outcome of his appeal of a death sentence for the murder of a St. Louis hotel clerk. He had previously killed a liquor store clerk after being released from a reformatory.

Federal authorities imposed a blackout on news about Hall's and Heady's stay on death row. Marshal Tatman announced that only three reporters—one representative each from the Associated Press, the United Press, and the International News Service—would be permitted to witness the execution. Before they could transmit their stories, they would have to debrief colleagues who worked for various accredited newspapers and magazines, as well as for radio and television stations. Also, none of the reporters would be allowed to use a prison telephone to inform the public of details of the kidnappers' death, and photographs of the execution would be prohibited.

Hall and Heady were served their first prison dinner around 7 P.M. on Friday, November 20. Asked if she was ready for supper, Heady replied, "I'd love it." The meal consisted of beef stew, navy beans, spinach, French fries, bread and butter, and black coffee. There was no dessert. Although she ate heartily, Hall sat down on his cot and rested for a time before eating.

On November 24, St. Louis police chief Jeremiah O'Connell received permission from federal authorities to question Hall and Heady one last time about the missing $303,720. The police wanted to ask him about several statements he made in his confession to the FBI that were later introduced at his trial. Those statements conflicted substantially with accounts by Shoulders regarding the circumstances surrounding Hall's arrest on October 6. Now that the St. Louis police had complete copies of Hall's confession, in which he claimed that neither of his suitcases had been taken to the Newstead station at the time of his arrest, O'Connell wanted to ask Hall about his references to a mysterious man he had seen in the corridor at the time of his arrest, and to a blonde woman he had seen sitting in a car parked outside the hotel at the time of his arrest. The FBI grudgingly granted its permission to O'Connell on condition that he alone interrogate Hall, since only he had made the request.

That evening, I. A. Long, president of the Board of Police Commissioners, telephoned James V. Bennett, director of the Federal Bureau of Prisons, and obtained permission for St. Louis circuit attorney Edward L. Dowd to join O'Connell in the interrogation, with two stenographers also sitting in, since it was likely that there would be other prosecutions related to the Greenlease case. An FBI agent arranged to meet O'Connell and Dowd in Jefferson City, and accompany them to the penitentiary.

Meanwhile, also on November 24, the FBI again questioned Dolan; and St. Louis chief of detectives James E. Chapman, Inspector George Parker, and O'Connell revisited the Town House. The Board of Police Commissioners announced that a departmental inquiry would formally question Shoulders, Dolan, and Hager about the missing ransom.

That same day, Roy Dietrich, Hall's lawyer, visited his client for the first time since his sentencing. Their meeting lasted three hours, and afterwards the lawyer told reporters, "He seems ready to go. Hall's attitude is one of resignation more than courage." Dietrich, who did not see Heady during his visit, also complained that Marshal Tatman had "whisked Hall out of jail without my knowing." Dietrich had gone to the Jackson County jail at 3 P.M. on the previous Friday to see Hall, only to discover that he and Heady had been taken to Jefferson City an hour earlier.

"Hall still doesn't realize what he did," Dietrich said, noting that Hall showed no indication that he wanted to appeal. "He tells me it was all a nightmare."

Explaining the purpose of his visit, Dietrich said, "My duties as a lawyer have ended; my duties as a man haven't. I told Hall that, as the clock ticks off his last twenty-four days, to realize no man actually knows how much time he has ahead of him."

Harold Hull, Heady's lawyer, and her aunt Nellie Baker had managed to visit with the condemned woman by arriving at the Jackson County jail a few hours prior to her transfer. The day marked the deadline for a motion for a new trial, and Heady reiterated her decision not to appeal.

Missouri governor Phil M. Donnelly said he continued to receive hundreds of requests for tickets to the execution of Hall and Heady, though he himself did not plan to attend. Arrangements for witnesses were in the hands of Marshal Tatman and the Federal Bureau of Prisons.

The *St. Louis Post-Dispatch*, in an editorial published November 25 titled "Where Did It Go?," articulated the sentiments of a great many people who still believed that Hall knew where the missing ransom was hidden. "Now that Hall is a condemned man," it said, "living in the death cell, ticking off the days until his end in a gas chamber, there is little reason for him to tell anything other than the truth. . . . Five weeks later, the mystery is bigger than ever."

Shoulders—one of four men who knew the answer to that mystery—had submitted his resignation from the police force to protest against the departmental inquiry, but that resignation still remained "in abeyance." He was still assigned to the Newstead district, but was not being paid.

The Kansas City federal grand jury inquiring into the whereabouts of the missing ransom twice called Costello to testify. On each occasion, he declined to account for his activities on the night of Tuesday, October 6—the night of Hall's arrest—insisting that the testimony might tend to incriminate him. St. Louis police had determined that, on that night, Costello had not appeared at his usual haunts. At 3:15 in the morning of Wednesday, October 7, during Hall's interrogation, a squad car had stopped Costello, who was driving a yellow Cadillac, on South Kingshighway—not far from his home—for routine questioning. Ace driver Joseph Travis was following him in a black Cadillac, also owned by Costello. Travis just happened to be the driver who claimed that he drove Hager to the Town House to rent an apartment for Hall. Hotel manager Jean Fletcher, of course, insisted that another man—not Hager—had rented the apartment.

Costello also refused to answer questions about his whereabouts on the night before Hall's and Heady's arrests.

Shoulders continued to insist publicly that he had a second tipster on Hall, in addition to Hager, while also stating that he would rather be killed or go to prison than reveal the informant's name—who, of course, was Costello, a close friend for twenty-five years. On October 15, the two men even went to Lambert-St. Louis Field, the city's airport, to pick up Shoulders's son, Louis Jr., who was flying in from Colorado after receiving his military discharge. The younger Shoulders had driven an Ace cab before going into the service. Moreover, when Costello was in Faith Hospital some years earlier for an operation, Shoulders and June Marie George, his so-called landlady, had gone to visit him.

Meanwhile, ex-cabdriver Hager moved to California. His wife claimed that he left because he wanted to avoid further questioning by investigators about the missing ransom, despite his insistence that he had told them all that he knew. It was true that he wanted to avoid further questioning. But it was his boss, Joe Costello, who had ordered him to leave town, and no doubt provided the necessary funds to underwrite the move, since Hager could not even afford to move into a bigger apartment with his wife, much less resettle in California.

Costello had good reason to want Hager far away. The cabbie's lies were the only thing protecting the mobster and the two policemen who had colluded with him in the theft of half of the ransom. Under relentless questioning, Costello feared, Hager might tell the truth. Since Hall was the only other person who knew at least some of the truth—and, improbably, was actually telling it—it seemed a safe bet that Costello's stonewalling, Shoulders's indignant insistence that he was being truthful, Dolan's corroboration of Shoulders's account out of fear for the well-being of his own family, and Hager's sudden departure for California might keep the authorities at bay until Hall and Heady were safely executed.

The FBI also questioned a prisoner named Charles Rasmussen, who had spent a night in the Jackson County jail, where Hall was also incarcerated, while being transferred from New Orleans to Minneapolis. The authorities had planted Rasmussen in the prison to obtain information from Hall. Rasmussen, in an all-too-transparent attempt to get some kind of quid pro quo leniency, claimed that Hall told him two other prisoners, Thomas Bordelon and Victor Linkletter, both being held for robbing safes, had received some of the ransom money from a Detroit underworld syndicate. Hall wanted Rasmussen to warn the two men that the money was "hot." Linkletter denied that he had ever received any of the money, or that he even knew Hall. However, a jail trusty reported that he saw Hall pass a note to Rasmussen on the night of November 1–2. Federal authorities later charged Rasmussen, a car theft suspect, with making false statements to the FBI.

While Rasmussen was attempting to manipulate the FBI in an effort to gain his freedom, several ordinary citizens tried to exploit the Greenlease family for financial gain. The FBI arrested four people on federal charges of plotting to defraud Robert C. Greenlease. Bennie Bruce Hatfield, an eighteen-year-old high school senior from Sedalia, Missouri, was charged with using the mail in an attempt to obtain $10,000 from the family in exchange for information about Bobby's whereabouts. Gerald T. Lambkins, also eighteen years old, of St. Joseph made three calls to the Greenlease home, while negotiations with Hall were underway, and demanded $50,000 in ransom; he also was arrested. A Philadelphia waitress named Betty Robbins was accused of trying to extort $4,000 from the boy's father through the mail. A few days later, another Philadelphia woman, Frances Keplin Fallaro, the mother of two children, was arrested and charged with writing an extortion letter demanding $25,000 from Bobby's father. Both Robbins and Fallaro claimed to be holding Bobby.

In a last-ditch attempt to discover where the missing half of the ransom was, Chief O'Connell and Circuit Attorney Dowd, accompanied by FBI agent Don Walters, finally met with Hall and Heady on November 30, just weeks before the execution. Their statements were taken in the legal form of a dying declaration.

"Well, I made my statement and the FBI has it," a somewhat exasperated Heady told O'Connell, "and it has been read at the trial and everything, and I don't think I have anything more to say at all."

But O'Connell and Dowd persisted in reviewing her and Hall's movements from the time they arrived in St. Louis until they rented the apartment. Although Heady continued to cooperate, many of her answers were variations on the same theme—she could not remember, because most of the time she was drunk. She could not even recall having gone to the bus station with Hall when they first arrived in St. Louis. As for Rasmussen's statement that Hall had told him about passing the bulk of his money to a Detroit syndicate, she said, "Don't you know that everybody wants to get in the act now? That they want to tell they knew something to get their name in the paper, or get a little attention?"

Heady also noted that both she and Hall planned to visit large cities such as New York and make small purchases in retail stores with the $10 and $20 bills, getting unmarked money as change.

She insisted that neither she nor Hall had been permitted to talk to any other prisoner, and that her and Hall's cells on death row were separated by three empty cells.

She also repeated once again that she and Hall knew that the ransom money would be marked. That was why they insisted on having it from all twelve Federal Reserve banks. They had never discussed selling it to a syndicate. Referring to Shoulders, she remarked, "He probably sold it to some syndicate for maybe half, or maybe a hundred thousand dollars. We heard that rumour. That's probably why they didn't find it on him, because he probably got rid of it to some syndicate."

Informed by Dowd that the police were "still very anxious" about finding the missing ransom, she said, "And so are we. And I didn't get a trip to Hawaii. That's what burns me up. Maybe somebody else is running around on something else you got for them."

So far as Heady was personally concerned, the biggest mystery surrounding the kidnapping and its aftermath was why Hall had behaved so unpredictably and even bizarrely after killing Bobby, when he had planned and rehearsed taking Bobby out of school down to the last detail.

"I can't figure out why he did any of the things he did," Heady admitted. "I can't figure out why he had left me in that apartment. I can't figure out why he starts running around in a taxicab. I wanted him to go right back home and stay there. He said no, 'Go to St. Louis.' I don't know why. I asked him, and he said he didn't know either; and the only thing I could figure out was he just got drunk and didn't have any sense. I've never got an explanation for it and I have wondered and wondered, why he went out there and started tossing [the money] around."

Heady was asked: "Will you give us any leads on that money, where it might be, even if it is just your opinion?"

She replied: "I think Shoulders has it."

For his part, Hall insisted once again that the two suitcases were not taken to the police station at the time of his arrival. He noted that Shoulders made no effort to determine if he had a weapon on him, but almost immediately asked for the keys to his luggage. After getting the keys, said Hall, Shoulders opened the closet and examined the two suitcases.

"They pushed me into an overstuffed chair," Hall said. "Imagine! A policeman with his experience letting me sit in a chair like that. It would have been one of the best places in the world to have a pistol stashed."

Hall also noted that he had not been handcuffed, and that both Shoulders and Dolan walked out of the hotel room ahead of him, and let him close the door.

During the four-hour interview, O'Connell and Dowd showed Hall a number of photographs, including those of Costello and other members of the criminal underworld, in an effort to identify the mysterious third man Hall saw standing outside his apartment talking to Shoulders on the night of his arrest. Hall was unable, though, to identify the man.

Hall also said that he once found Sandra O'Day holding keys to his suitcases containing the ransom when the two of them were spending the night of October 5 at the Coral Court. He had hidden the keys in a pillowcase while napping, and when he questioned O'Day about how she found the keys, she explained that they had just "slipped out" and she was looking at them out of curiosity.

"I was afraid of being rolled," Hall said, adding that he had tried to persuade Hager and O'Day that he did not really have much money on him. "They were beginning to ask a lot of questions about the money. Once I opened a suitcase at Coral Court, but I don't think Sandra saw me."

In a jocular moment, a complacent Hall even told O'Connell and Dowd, "The food is very good here. You've heard of these guys they have to carry to the gas chamber. Well, if I keep gaining weight, they'll just roll me in."

Neither Hall nor Heady was allowed a radio in their cells, but on Sunday each was given a newspaper to read.

While Hall and Heady counted down the days leading to their execution, the search for the missing ransom continued to be front-page news in St. Louis and Kansas City, where the federal grand jury was scheduled to resume its investigation on December 14, a Monday. Subpoenas were issued to four St. Louis policemen who were in the Newstead Avenue station on the night of Hall's arrest, but who reportedly did not see Shoulders bring in the kidnappers' two suitcases containing the ransom.

During this period, Shoulders asked Chief O'Connell for police protection, saying that there had been threats on his life. When an inspector interviewed the suspended detective at his North Side home on 5382 Wabada Avenue, however, Shoulders declined to reveal how the threats were conveyed, and noted that he had not asked for around-the-clock protection. Rather, he simply wanted a detective to accompany him whenever he left home, because he sensed that he was being followed. O'Connell described Shoulders as being "non-cooperative" in his interview with Parker. Shoulders had only recently returned from his trip to Hawaii with his landlady, June Marie George.

A few days before the grand jury reconvened, the newspapers also reported that the "mysterious blonde woman" had surfaced and was being questioned by police in connection with the missing ransom. The police refused to identify the woman, for her protection, but revealed that she had been seated in an automobile parked near the door when Hall and the two policemen emerged from Hall's Town House apartment. She had gone to the hotel on a visit. Hall had noticed her when he was being led out, and later told the police that she had short blond hair and was seated in a light grey or tan Oldsmobile. In her statement to the police, the woman corroborated Hall's account that neither Shoulders nor Dolan was carrying a suitcase when the group left the apartment.

Walter H. McDowell, a clerk at the Newstead station, also told St. Louis assistant chief Joseph E. Casey that, after reflecting on the matter of the missing ransom for some days, he had remembered seeing a policeman carrying a suitcase walk through the front door of the station house approximately one hour and twenty minutes after Hall had been booked. Hall had been booked at 8:57 P.M. Earlier, McDowell had told federal agents that he had not been in a position to see whether Hall's suitcases had been brought into the station.

Late in the afternoon of Thursday, December 10, St. Louis Board of Police president I. A. Long summoned reporters to his office and handed them a statement saying that he was suspending patrolman Elmer Dolan, pending a hearing, on charges of conduct unbecoming an officer and dereliction of duty. He also said that charges would soon be filed against Shoulders. Although neither charge against Dolan was of a criminal nature, the suspension made front-page news around the country the next day. Stunned by the suspension, Dolan said, "What can I say? I'm not accused of anything. If I were, I'd make a statement. I'm not hiding."

Shoulders merely laughed when he learned of the board's actions, saying, "Why, I'm no longer a policeman, and haven't been since the twenty-fourth of October." Reminded that his resignation had not been accepted, he retorted, "They stopped my pay, and that's enough for me."

But in the wake of the Board of Police charges, a desperate Shoulders changed his story. On December 12, testifying before the federal grand jury, he now asserted that he had kept Hall's luggage in his car until after Hall was booked. Shoulders's explanation was that he did not want "any gassy policemen" discussing the case at that time. He explained that he had left the two suitcases in the police car while Hall was being booked, at 8:57 P.M., and had not brought them in until ten minutes later. But several policemen and other witnesses who were at the station when Hall arrived contradicted Shoulders's revised version. No witness had been found who saw either of the two policemen make a second trip into the station with the suitcases. Originally, Shoulders had also claimed that one suitcase was transported in the police car and the other in the automobile driven by cabdriver John Hager. Now he said that both suitcases were brought in the police car. Shoulders also challenged the Board of Police to make public the transcript of his statements at the departmental inquiry into the missing ransom.

Hager had followed behind the police car en route to the station, Shoulders said. But Dolan told his superiors that he did not see Hager following the automobile at any time.

Shoulders's landlady, June Marie George, had also changed her unlisted number to another unlisted number two days after the kidnappers were arrested. The police wanted to know why.

When the federal grand jury reconvened on December 14, it was faced with the challenge of trying to answer several unresolved questions related to the missing ransom:

- What did Shoulders do from 3:30 P.M., Tuesday, October 6, when he got his first tip on Hall, until 7:30 P.M., when the arrest was made?
- Where was Shoulders when he left the Newstead Avenue station after Hall was booked at 8:57 P.M., until he returned at 10:40 P.M.?
- Why did he pick patrolman Dolan, a uniformed beat patrolman and until recently a member of the vice squad, to accompany him to the Town House to arrest Hall?
- Where was the stakeout that Shoulders said he was on when the desk sergeant called him at 7:05 P.M.?
- Why did Shoulders neglect to handcuff Hall when he arrested him at the Town House?
- Who were the mysterious persons hanging around the Town House on the night Hall was there?
- Why had Shoulders now changed his story regarding the suitcases containing the ransom?
- Was the suitcase seen being brought into the police station one hour and twenty minutes after Hall was booked one of those belonging to the kidnapper?

Three St. Louisans were the first witnesses to testify: FBI agent Frank Staab; John Sakellarios, chef at the Congress Hotel; and grocer Max Wolff. The mystery blonde was also identified as Viola Freeny, a former cashier at the Town House, who had left that job three months prior to her testimony.

Other witnesses scheduled to testify included seventeen-year-old Barbara Cupp, who was in the Newstead station, waiting for a friend, when Shoulders entered on the night of Hall's arrest; Walter McDowell, the clerk in the station who saw Dolan walk in with a suitcase one hour and twenty minutes after Hall was booked; and FBI agent John Bush.

Katharine G. Overstreet, a switchboard operator at the Town House when Hall was a guest, testified that she was on duty October 6 when she saw Dolan, accompanied by another man who was not in uniform, take the elevator to the third floor shortly after 10 P.M. When they returned a short time later, Dolan was carrying a man's straw hat, a belt, and a whisky bottle. She recalled that the manager, Jean Fletcher, had asked what the trouble was, and Dolan replied that it was nothing but a routine investigation. Hager told reporters that he was the man who accompanied Dolan, and that they had gone to look for a pistol.

Shown the two suitcases and the briefcase used by Hall, Max Wolff, who operated a grocery store across from the Town House, told the grand jury that he had seen three men hurry out of the building carrying three suitcases on October 6. But he was unable to identify the luggage, saying he had seen the bags too long ago to have any distinct memory of what they looked like.

Wolff also declared that neither man with Shoulders was Dolan or Hager, however. He was able to establish the time as "shortly before" 9 P.M. because he had watched the start of the Veiled Prophet Ball on television—an annual society event. The next morning, he told Jean Fletcher, manager of the Town House, "I saw money being taken out of here last night." He told a reporter that he had just parked his car in an apartment garage and was walking to his apartment on Union Boulevard when he saw the three men exit the Town House. "I was right in front of the place, and I'm sure one of the men was Shoulders. He was in civilian clothes, had on a black tie, and was wearing tortoiseshell glasses. I was within two feet of him and the lighting was good. He was carrying a shiny black suitcase. He crossed to the north side of Pershing to a car parked there. The other two men cut across the lawn and walked east to the southwest corner of Union and Pershing. They were also in civilian clothes but were smaller than Shoulders. Neither was handcuffed. One man carried a two-suiter piece of luggage. The other had an ordinary size suitcase and a briefcase." By "two-suiter piece of luggage," Wolff apparently meant the large green footlocker.

On the same day that the grand jury reconvened, the *Post-Dispatch* revealed that Shoulders was seeking a permit from the St. Louis Police Department to carry a pistol. He had requested the application form the previous Saturday, saying that his life had been threatened, but without providing any details.

Also that day, Shoulders's wife, Florence Shoulders, filed a petition for divorce. She and Shoulders had been married since 1927. Mrs. Shoulders declared that her husband deserted her without cause on September 2, 1952. They had three grown children. Circuit judge James F. Nangle declined to issue an immediate decree, as was customary, indicating that he was taking judicial notice of Shoulders's intention to marry June Marie George. His wife was asking for $300 a month in alimony, and for her estranged husband to assume the remainder of her mortgage debt.

Governor Donnelly reported that he had received between twenty and twenty-five requests, mostly from nonresidents of Missouri, urging him to grant clemency to Hall and Heady. Some wanted the execution to be delayed until after Christmas. Donnelly noted that he did not have authority in the matter. Since the crime was a federal one, President Eisenhower was the only person who could grant clemency to the kidnappers. Authorities did note, however, that a telephone was inside the death house, just a short distance from the gas chamber, in the event the president gave the condemned pair a last-minute reprieve. Officials noted that the telephone had saved only one condemned man since the chamber was built. The last prisoner to create any disturbance was Adam

Richetti, a gangster associate of the late Pretty Boy Floyd, who had been convicted for his role in the Kansas City Union Station Massacre of June 1933. On October 7, 1938, when the door of the Missouri gas chamber closed on him, the twenty-seven-year-old murderer had screamed and cringed as he waited for the sodium cyanide pellets to drop into the jar of acid beneath his chair.

As the day of their execution drew near, both Hall and Heady remained calm. Outside the prison, residents of Jefferson City decorated their stores and homes, shopped for presents, and prepared for Christmas. Inside, the grim preparations for the execution proceeded apace. Both Hall and Heady were asked what they wanted for their last meal, and both gave identical answers— fried chicken, mashed potatoes and gravy, a combination salad with Roquefort dressing, and orange or pineapple sherbet. Neither asked for a beverage.

Father Evans reported that he would be with Hall during his final hours, and his curate, Father Bull, with Heady. "I want you to stay with me until the very end," Father Evans quoted Hall as telling him.

Hall spent much of his last hours reading Wild West magazines, while Heady seemed devoted to working crossword puzzles in the daily newspapers. Both had put on weight—Hall about twenty pounds, and Heady about five. Heady even joked about the roll of fat she said Hall had gained around his midriff. Neither had been given the opportunity to do any exercise, apart from walking around their cells.

Yet again, on the afternoon before he was to be executed, Hall insisted that he had all of the ransom money at the time of his arrest. In a final conference with Dietrich, he also assumed full responsibility for the kidnapping and murder of Bobby Greenlease, and denied that he ever had any intention of killing Heady. Dietrich also offered his opinion on the matter, saying that he thought Heady remained "still loyal" to Hall. The attorney told reporters that he had visited Hall at the kidnapper's request.

"I believe in an infinite God," Dietrich said, after the meeting, "and if I felt that I could give any help to Hall, I would be glad to do so. Although he knew what he was doing, he was drinking so heavily and taking Benzedrine to such an extent his sense of right and wrong was dulled."

Dietrich also revealed that Hall was halfway through reading *The World's First Love* by Bishop Fulton J. Sheen, a popular Catholic preacher.

Prison officials, though, were quick to observe that Hall had told more than one fellow prisoner—most likely trustees serving his meals—that his only regret was that he had doomed himself by going on a drunken spree after arriving in St. Louis. "It was a life or death proposition with me," a prison official quoted Hall as saying. "I had intended to sit on that money for five to ten years if necessary, then fence it. If I had a chance, I'd never have been taken alive. I didn't intend to be. Those cops made me sit in a chair and they caught me away from my gun."

On the morning before Hall was scheduled to die, John Downs, the prosecuting attorney from Buchanan County, Missouri, visited Hall to see whether he was involved in the murder the previous August of Mary Jane Nester, a wealthy Nodaway County resident. He was accompanied by Sergeant Jack Inman of the state highway patrol. Hall told Downs, "If it would please you, I could attest to anything. But I know you don't want that, and it wouldn't do anyone any good."

Hall also told Downs, "I hope God doesn't judge me as harshly as society."

Downs also interviewed Heady, who appeared embarrassed when the prosecutor found her with her hair up in curlers and wearing a pink housecoat.

"I'm sorry you came before I had time to dress," she said.

Heady also told Downs that she was concerned about what would happen to Doc, her pet boxer. Unable to find a home for him, she had considered putting him to sleep, but changed her mind after receiving too many complaints from those who opposed that idea.

As the prosecutor was leaving, she asked him, "Aren't you going to ask me about the money?"

"No," Downs replied.

"Well, everyone else has," she retorted.

Heady also had another visitor on the day before the execution— St. Louis Food and Drug agent Roy Pruitt, who asked her about the supply of drugs—mostly amphetamines—found in her purse at the time of her arrest. Pruitt had, in fact, gone to both Heady's and Hall's cells the previous day, while accompanied by an FBI agent, and both refused to talk with the FBI agent present. Now Heady told Pruitt that she could tell him about the drugs, and added mysteriously, "Carl can tell you all about the money, too."

Pruitt arranged for Heady to be brought into the corridor outside Hall's cell, and she then urged him to talk about the ransom and the drugs. He said to her, "Shut up. We have already talked too much. Remember, we never rat on a pal."

After Pruitt took her back to her cell, he asked her, "Why didn't you tell me you knew about the pills and the ransom money?"

She replied, "Carl and I have a pact. I cannot talk about the drugs or the money without his permission. And he has refused to give it to me. My lips are sealed."

That was her—and Hall's—final word about the missing ransom.

One of Heady's last requests was that she be allowed to wear her golden slippers, which were brought to her.

On the same day that Dietrich visited his client, the grand jury in Kansas City heard testimony from Esther Wells, who had been at the Newstead station on the night of October 6, shortly before Shoulders and Dolan arrived with Hall. At the moment when Hall was brought in, Wells had gone to a nearby store to place a long-distance telephone call; her testimony was important because it allowed the grand jury to fix the time of Hall's arrival. As Wells returned to the station, she testified, she saw both Shoulders and Dolan leaving.

While Hall and Heady prepared for death on the day of their execution, the grand jury in Kansas City indicted a tormented Elmer Dolan on perjury charges. The indictment charged Dolan with committing perjury in testimony given before the grand jury on October 30, when he was asked about his movements and those of Shoulders on the night of October 6, when they arrested Hall and Heady. The grand jury also handed down five other indictments, but U.S. Attorney Scheufler refused to say whether they were related to the Greenlease case or not. He did indicate, though, that Shoulders was not among those indicted. The grand jury then went into recess until December 29.

The indictment of Dolan charged that under questioning by Assistant U.S. Attorney Kenneth C. West, Dolan was asked the following questions and gave the following answers:

Q. When did you first know that there were two suitcases involved in this case?

A. After I got to the police station.

Q. Did you take them out?

A. I took one of them out, and Lt. Shoulders took the other one out.

Q. Was this immediately after you got to the station?

A. Right after I got to the station; the lieutenant was going into the station with the prisoner and I had taken one of the suitcases out.

Q. Where was the other suitcase?

A. In the police car.

Q. And the briefcase?

A. I had the briefcase with me, too.

Q. You had a suitcase and a briefcase?

A. Yes, sir.

Q. And the other one was still in the police car?

A. Yes, sir.

Q. Where did you take those?

A. Back in to Lt. Shoulders' office.

Q. Was that the same time you went in with Hall, roughly?

A. Hall was already in the station then.

Dolan, who had been sitting in the anteroom of the grand jury chambers waiting to testify, was placed under arrest immediately after the indictment was handed down. Scheufler explained that the policeman had been subpoenaed in order to give him the opportunity to change his testimony. The patrolman, clearly more afraid of being killed by Shoulders or Costello than of going to prison, was held pending bail of $25,000.

9.

Goodbye and Thanks

On the morning of Heady's last day, Nellie Baker, who was clearly showing signs of strain, visited her niece in her cell. Heady's defence attorney, Harold Hull, accompanied her.

"Bonnie acted quite natural," Baker said. "She always had a way of facing up to things and taking them as they come."

Since this was the first time a man and a woman would be executed simultaneously, prison officials were also making an exception on how the two prisoners would be dressed. The officials now decided that Heady and Hall would be permitted to wear their usual prison garb when they were strapped into their chairs.

Hall and Heady were allowed to be together twice on their last day. A small table was placed in the corridor just outside Hall's cell. During their midday meal, she sat on a chair and he sat on the edge of his cot, reaching through the bars to eat. Marshal Tatman sat nearby. They talked for about thirty minutes, and held hands for a part of that time. Tatman later told reporters, "I made no attempt to overhear their conversation, but they appeared happy and eager to see each other."

Marshall Hoag, the lawyer from Pleasanton and longtime friend of the Hall family, was a late-afternoon visitor. He had agreed to claim Hall's body, and declined to reveal when and where the funeral service and burial would be.

Hull told reporters that private graveside services would be held for Heady in Clearmont, Missouri, at a time to be decided by Baker. At five o'clock, they both left for the return trip to St. Joseph.

Hall and Heady also each spent two hours—from 3 to 5 P.M.—meeting privately with a priest. Hall talked with Father Evans, and Heady met with his assistant, Father Bull. Father Evans asked Hall about the story published in the *St. Louis Globe-Democrat* that quoted Shoulders as saying that Hall told him he planned to kill Heady soon after he collected the $600,000 ransom.

"That's absolutely false," Hall replied. "It never entered my mind. If it had, I would have had plenty of time to do it in."

He went on: "I wish you would tell the newspaper people for me to please state that this was never in my mind. I want to refute those accusations made by Shoulders and others."

Hall also revealed that he was trying to keep Heady's spirits up, even though he had appeared to be the gloomy one, while she had often seemed almost unconcerned about her impending fate.

"She's proud," he said. "She doesn't want to break."

Asked about the rumour that Hall planned to kill her, Heady was equally dismissive, saying, "Why would he want to kill me?"

Father Bull pointed out to her that she had been seen taking Bobby from the French Institute of Notre Dame de Sion, and had been the only person who could identify Hall as her accomplice.

"That isn't true," Heady insisted. "I love Carl, and Carl loves me."

Hall claimed that he had "only pity for Shoulders and Hager," the crooked detective who arrested him and the taxi driver who betrayed him.

The two priests left the prison to have dinner at a downtown hotel. Before eating, they read the "Prayer for Prisoners" from *The Book of Common Prayer* for Hall and Heady.

The condemned pair ate their last meal at five o'clock. Both ate heartily. Marshal Tatman, state corrections director Whitecotton, and two guards stood about five feet away, but could not hear what they were saying. Tatman and his wife later visited the couple, who said both were satisfied with the food and had no complaints.

Shortly before 9 P.M., Father Evans and Father Bull returned to the prison for a final visit with the condemned pair. The two priests would remain with Hall and Heady until the end. Hall told Father Evans that he saw the hand of God in his arrest.

"I can see good in this, Father," Hall confided. "I only killed Bobby. If I had had just twelve hours more, I would have killed five more. God saved me from that."

Did Hall mean five people who had already been identified with the case? the priest asked.

"Oh, no," Hall said. "I mean five that I've hated all my life. I'd have got them, too. With all the money, it would have been easy. See what I mean, I killed only one, and was caught. It might have been six, five more." After pausing for a moment, he then emphatically declared, "That's the working of Christ. It had to be. I had murder in my heart. God knew, and saved those five others."

Lighting a cigarette, he added reflectively, "I'm glad. And you can do something for me, Father. Tell the world. Tell them that only God is important. I know now. And tell them that if it weren't for whisky, those penitentiaries would be closed. Tell the world, Father. Look, if Christ could do this for me—a mean, drunken, miserable so-and-so—Christ could do it for anybody. I know."

Hall denied that his death cell conversion was prompted by a fear of death.

"Father, I'm an intelligent man," he said. "This isn't a conversion because I'm afraid of death. I've never been afraid of death. All my life I've been wondering, thinking. And if it made sense to intelligent men all over the world, there must be something to it."

He then repeated his desire to have the world know that he had become an instrument of Christ's will.

"Why do we have to wait so long?" he asked. "Why do we have to be so stupid? Since I've been in jail, I know it was the will of Christ that I couldn't kill those other five. He stopped me after killing Bobby. And now I'm ready for God, my judge. And I'm glad."

Was Bonnie equally repentant? Father Evans asked.

"Sure. She'll tell you. She loves me, and I love her. I know her better than anyone else. Bonnie was drunk for a year. I was drunk daily for months. After a while, anything seems all right. I'm the guilty one. She couldn't say no to me. The only sin she was guilty of was loving me."

Hall then asked the time. Told that it was around 9 P.M., he laughed.

"I haven't got long to live, Father," he said. "Not here, anyway. And I'm looking forward to meeting my judge."

Around 11 P.M., less than an hour before she would be led to the gas chamber, Heady declared to Father Bull, "I'm not going to go down there crying. Of course, we're both sorry for this horrible crime. We want to be forgiven. But then these crusaders come around and ask me to say it was whisky, and I won't go for those crusaders."

Hall, of course, had already placed the blame squarely on his drinking.

"I used to go to church in Maryville," Heady went on. "I'd see a man who'd had a date with a blonde the night before. Hypocrites. It would be a lot better if he'd leave the blonde alone, and stay with his wife. That's why I left the church."

Father Bull pointed out that Jesus had come to redeem all sinners, including hypocrites.

"Yes," she replied, "but I don't like hypocrites. Carl doesn't either."

Some moments after eleven o'clock, Father Evans administered Holy Unction—the sacrament of the sick and the dying—by anointing Hall's and Heady's foreheads with oil, and presented each of them with a crucifix.

At 11:25 P.M., the telephone rang on death row. That was the signal that the condemned pair were to be taken on their last walk. Deputy Marshal Marvin Rowland, accompanied by two prison guards, entered Hall's cell. Marshal Tatman, his wife, and a prison guard proceeded the other thirty feet to Heady's. With a loud rasp, the master security locks were unbolted, and the two cell doors swung open.

Heady had prepared for her death as though she were making her last public appearance on a stage, and wanted to look her best. By the time the marshals arrived to escort her and Hall from their cells, she was primped and ready. Most condemned prisoners were given a haircut before their execution, but Heady's long hair was neatly done up. She had also applied lipstick and donned a bright green regulation prison dress and her pair of bedroom slippers. Hall's hair was also rather long. He, too, was dressed in regulation prison attire—an olive green twill shirt, matching cotton trousers with a black stripe down the sides, and black laceless shoes. He was not wearing socks, and Heady was not wearing nylons. When Heady complained about the cold, Mrs. Tatman draped her short black Persian wool coat over Heady's shoulders. Both prisoners, each wearing manacles attached to wide leather straps around their waists, went willingly. It was 11:28.

Separated by about ten feet, the two groups walked down the sixteen-cell death row. Samuel Norbert Reese, the twenty-one-year-old convicted murderer who occupied the last cell, had composed a poem commemorating the execution entitled "Thoughts While Sitting in the Gas Chambers." He had tried, but without success, to persuade guards to show it to the condemned pair.

Climbing the seven stone steps to the ground-level landing, the group pushed through the double doors of B hall and into the cold night. The stars were clearly visible in a cloudless sky, and the temperature stood at a frigid seven degrees.

The prison yard was draped with Christmas trimmings, and a fir tree was strung with brightly coloured lights. In one cell block, "Gloria in Excelsis Deo"—the ancient hymn that began with the words, "Glory to God in the highest, and on earth, peace to men of good will"—blared from a radio. Some streets in downtown Jefferson City had been blocked off so that several churches could hold their annual Christmas procession. Lafayette Street, the main thoroughfare leading to the penitentiary, was roped off to keep curious spectators away from the prison gates.

"It's colder out here than I thought it was," Hall said to his guards.

In the light of the yard, both Hall and Heady could easily be seen by some of the other prisoners, and a few began calling and jeering at them.

"Bye, Bonnie," one of them shouted, and several others took up the refrain. Another prisoner called out, "Pour it on 'em."

In general, though, the majority of the twenty-five hundred prisoners seemed uninterested in the unfolding drama. All was quiet within the prison, as on any normal night. During previous executions, the prisoners were known to rattle their cell bars when a condemned man was led to the gas chamber. That afternoon, the prison guard had been doubled to 150; and another thirty-five highway patrolmen, most of them in civilian clothes, were stationed both inside and outside the walls. In addition, more than sixty patrolmen within a hundred-mile radius were on standby; and police were also operating two-way radios at locations considered vulnerable either to a riot or a demonstration by the public, including the prison's railroad and garage gates, and two downtown intersections—Capitol and Cherry streets, and Capitol and Lafayette streets. The prison population had also been locked in their cells immediately after supper, and lights had gone out at ten o'clock.

Two cars were waiting. Heady, still wearing Mrs. Tatman's black coat, stepped into the first, along with Marshal and Mrs. Tatman. Hall and two deputy marshals got into the second car.

The route to the gas chamber led down a five-hundred-yard road that wound past the prison yard and the plumbing shop, and then followed along the edge of the athletic field, which was ablaze with searchlights. Guards had been placed around the gas chamber, and other guards in the watchtowers were on alert to ensure that no prison outbreak or other violence interfered with the orderly implementation of the death sentence. Thousands of letters had flowed into Jefferson City, some bitterly congratulating the state for imposing the death penalty on the pair so swiftly. By now, an estimated ten thousand people had asked to witness the execution. Yet some letters also urged Heady and Hall to ask for forgiveness and repent for their sins. At least fifty people had written Governor Phil Donnell urging him to grant the pair clemency, even though he did not have the authority to do so. All of those letters were turned over to the federal government. Heady and Hall were not allowed to read any of them.

The thirty-two people who were to witness the execution—including the eighteen official witnesses—walked behind the two automobiles.

C. O. Parker, a prison official who drove the car that carried Hall, later said, "He walked right in with no hesitation. He did not appear tense or excited." Heady struck those who escorted her as being "very spry."

The trip lasted scarcely a minute. Hall and Heady then remained in the two automobiles for several minutes. At 11:35 they walked across a large stone cross embedded in the ground; a few withered roses still drooped from an overhead trellis. The doomed pair, their guards, penitentiary officials, doctors, and newsmen entered through one door, while the official witnesses to the execution walked through another. Hall and Heady were led into a detention room, and Father Evans and Father Bull soon joined them. Hall and

Heady appeared remarkably calm and reconciled to their grisly fate, talking animatedly, smoking, and at one point apparently laughing, perhaps over a shared joke.

The death house, a small limestone building built in 1937, measured about thirty square feet, with a forty-foot-long exhaust pipe protruding from the roof. It consisted of two small doorless rooms on one side, and the gas chamber on the other. One of the rooms was used to detain the condemned while the gas chamber was being prepared. The second room contained the vats into which the sulphuric acid would be poured, and the leather straps used to restrain the condemned.

The airtight gas chamber was painted white. The two perforated steel chairs reserved for Hall and Heady stood side by side. Conduits beneath each chair would soon be connected to three-gallon lead vats filled with sulphuric acid. When a lever was pulled, sodium cyanide pellets were dropped into the vats to create lethal hydrogen cyanide gas. After the execution, the gas was extracted through the exhaust pipe. Missouri was one of only nine states to use lethal gas as a method of execution. This was to be the first double execution in the state's history, and Heady was to become the first woman ever executed in the United States for kidnapping, and the only woman executed by lethal gas.

In the detention room, Director Whitecotton read the official execution order to Hall, while Marshal Tatman read the same order to Heady. Prison and federal officials stepped out of the cells at 11:45 to allow the two priests time to visit and pray with the pair. Father Evans said a psalm aloud, and led the couple in the "Our Father." As Hall and Heady held hands, despite the cuffs, they also confessed their sins one last time and received absolution.

Hall and Heady were then allowed to spend a few minutes together, sitting side by side on a cot, with Marshal Tatman on a chair in front of them.

"You wouldn't want to deprive them of that," Tatman later remarked.

The pair held hands and talked casually, and Hall, who had lit his last cigarette, leaned over at one point to give Heady a puff. Heady seemed animated, and even laughed at some remark by Tatman. They also kissed.

In the adjoining room, the guards were mixing sulphuric acid and water, as the witnesses watched.

Then three guards entered the cell and ordered the two prisoners to stand. At 11:55, Hall was ordered to remove his shoes, and Heady took off her slippers.

"Okay, out of the way," a deputy marshal ordered.

"See you later," Father Evans said to Bonnie.

"Sure," she said. "Thank you, Father."

"See you later, Carl," the priest said.

"You bet you will, Father," Hall replied.

While Heady watched, an official placed a blindfold on Hall, and then secured it at the back with a double strap. Mrs. Tatman then did the same with Heady. Guards and matrons led them into the gas chamber, with Hall going first.

"Please be careful and don't let me fall," Heady complained. "I can't see a thing."

The two metal chairs in the small, octagonal enclosure stood only a foot apart. Each prisoner was guided onto a steel chair, and the guards drew a series of straps tautly across each of their wrists, arms, chests, thighs, and ankles. Hall was strapped into the chair on Heady's right. His mouth was smeared with lipstick where Heady had kissed him one last time.

Heady complained that the straps on her arms and legs were too tight, and futilely tried to pull the hem of her skirt over her knees.

"It's tight," she said jokingly. "I'm not going anywhere."

She asked Hall if he had plenty of room, but he was breathing hard as the straps were being tightened and he did not answer.

Just before the iron door was closed, she asked Hall, "Are you doing all right, honey?"

"Yes, mama," he replied, still breathing heavily, and licking his lips.

"Is my dress pulled down?" Heady asked.

No one answered.

Two burly guards in shirtsleeves carried a vat filled with sulphuric acid into the chamber, and placed it under Hall's chair with a clang that made spectators jump. Two minutes later, they placed a similar vat under Heady's chair. The acid had cost the state a total of $4.40.

Marshal Tatman entered the chamber and asked them if either had anything further to confess about the whereabouts of the missing ransom money. Both shook their heads to indicate that they did not. Heady said, "No." Turning to Tatman, she added, "Goodbye and thanks."

She also addressed Assistant Deputy Warden Bernard Poiry, who had taken the pair their food during the four weeks they spent on death row. He had also helped to adjust the straps restraining Heady.

"Goodbye, Mr. Poiry," she said, "and thanks for everything."

Poiry clumsily shook hands with the pair, and Heady thanked him a second time.

Tatman, his wife, and the others quickly exited, and the guards shut the heavy doors. Then they turned the six pressure wheels until the chamber was sealed. The eighteen official witnesses took their places outside the glass panels. Some of the observers, sitting side by side only five feet away from the death chamber, had no trouble reading Heady's and Hall's lips as they spoke their last words.

"Carl."

"Yeah."

"Carl, I love you."

"I love you, Bonnie."

Hall also appeared to be mumbling to himself, and some observers assumed that he was praying.

At 12:02 A.M., Warden Ralph Eidson slowly pulled the lever, tripping a mechanism inside the chamber that dropped granular cyanide pellets from shelves under each chair into the vats of sulphuric acid. Whitish fumes instantly spiralled upwards from the cauldrons. Heady fought death by holding her breath, and kept her head upright. But Hall's fell forward as the clouds filled the chamber. The clouding was unusually dense because a double dose of the cyanide had been required for the execution.

Throughout the execution, Father Evans and Father Bull continued to read prayers for the repose of the souls of the two prisoners.

Hall was declared dead at 12:12 A.M., December 18, 1953, and Heady two minutes later. After death was certain, the blowers were turned on, forcing the gas out through the exhaust pipe, and ammonium hydroxide was pumped in as a neutralizer to the lethal fumes.

Dr. William V. McKnelly, and his assistant, Dr. G. Donald Shull, first pronounced Hall and Heady dead unofficially by looking at the corpses through the window. As soon as guards determined that it was safe to go into the chamber, the two physicians entered wearing gas masks and gloves. They checked for Hall's and Heady's heartbeats and reflexes and officially pronounced them dead.

Dr. Shull explained to the press that death was caused by inhalation of the gas fumes, causing a block in the exchange of oxygen from the arteries to body tissue. The tissue died from anoxia, with the central nervous system and the brain the first to be affected.

A quarter of an hour later, the bodies were removed, wrapped in plastic sheets—similar to the one, as several witnesses remarked, that Hall and Heady had wrapped Bobby's lifeless body in when they buried him.

Norbert O'Neill, the friend and business associate of Robert C. Greenlease, Bobby's father, was one of the witnesses, and had to avert his eyes when the cyanide was released into the chamber.

"But the thing that kept me going through the whole ordeal was the picture before my eyes of Bobby struggling with those two horrible creatures," he later told a reporter.

Robert Ledterman, who had helped to deliver the ransom money, was not a witness. Earlier in the day, he had sent word to the authorities of his decision to decline the invitation.

Reporters asked Warden Eidson if prison officials had administered sedatives to Hall and Heady before they were led to the gas chamber.

"It may be done in some institutions," he replied, "but definitely it is not done in ours."

The three newsmen permitted to witness the execution were Larry Hall, chief of the Associated Press bureau in Jefferson City; Ward Colwell, chief of the southwestern division of United Press, Kansas City; and James Kilgallon, a writer for the International News Service. They briefed the other members of the press— nearly one hundred in all—in the prison garage near the administration building immediately after the execution.

Other witnesses included Bernard Brannon, Kansas City chief of police; Arvid Owsley, sheriff of Jackson County; and George D. Spence, a North Kansas City patrolman who was one of Hall's guards in Kansas City. All had been invited by Tatman. Hall's witnesses, in addition to Father Evans, Hoag, and Dietrich, included R. C. Travis of Odessa, Missouri, who several years previously had travelled to California with Hall; Robert Moore of Kansas City; and Gerald Livingston, another North Kansas City patrolman who had guarded Hall. Heady's witness list contained only two names: Harold Hull and Father Bull, her legal and spiritual counsellors.

Dietrich, who had visited his client the day before the execution, told reporters that Hall insisted that he had revealed everything he knew about the missing ransom money. " 'Nobody got the money away from me until I was arrested,' " he quoted Hall as saying.

Dietrich also said that a prison matron posted outside Heady's cell told him that the prisoner "inspires me with her courage—with the apparent belief she has that she will go serenely to pay the price."

Father Evans, who was with the couple until the last, also confirmed for reporters that Hall and Heady were both "absolutely and completely reconciled. They were equally calm."

"She was upset because she couldn't look her best," Father Bull added. "She was disturbed because she couldn't wear fine clothes, because she had no fingernail polish, and because her hair was not the way she would have liked to have it."

Marshall Hoag, the lawyer from Pleasanton, Kansas, who had come to claim Hall's body, and who witnessed the execution, told reporters, "I never saw such resignation. It was wonderful. Wonderful to really accept Christ like that."

Sammy Reese, now the sole occupant on death row, went back to sleep an hour after the execution. His sentence was later commuted to two consecutive life terms.

At midnight, a traffic jam had formed outside the prison as curiosity seekers gathered to watch. Highway patrolmen and auxiliary police spent fifteen minutes dispersing the crowd. An hour later, two hearses removed the bodies to the Buescher Funeral Home, about three blocks away. By now the streets in Jefferson City were virtually empty.

Prison officials also inspected Hall's and Heady's cells in B building. As Reese dozed, they entered cell number 25, where Hall had spent his last hours. Several paperbacks lay on the green-and-black-striped mattress, including *I, the Jury* and *The Big Kill*, two murder mysteries by Mickey Spillane, a favourite author of Heady (she and Hall had exchanged several books); *Sartoris*, by William Faulkner; *Excuse It, Please!* by Cornelia Otis Skinner; and, under the mattress, *God Goes to Murderer's Row*, sent to Hall by a St. Louis woman who admonished him in an accompanying note to read it.

The author was M. Raymond, OCSO, a Trappist monk. The dust jacket copy read in part: "The hound of Heaven stalks the death house in pursuit of the soul of a modern Dismas in this true story of a doomed criminal who found God in the solitude of a prison." Also under the mattress were a black leather-bound copy of the New Testament and a ream of ruled notebook paper, which Tatman quickly picked up and flipped through.

"There's nothing in here," he announced. "Just blank papers."

"The tiny room, with painted yellow walls, like the others, and harshly lighted," still seemed almost occupied, noted one of the visitors, reporter James Scott of the *Star*. "A tooth brush, a comb, and two pencils were on the wash basin. A fresh tube of toothpaste was beside them."

Heady's cell, by contrast, revealed a hitherto unknown talent for art. On the wall next to her cot, she had drawn a two-foot figure of a baseball player wearing an old-fashioned uniform with striped socks. "The player had a magnificent moustache and bristling hair," Scott recorded. "His right hand grasped a heavy baseball bat, which touched an imaginary ground-line, and his left hand held a baseball over his head, ready to throw."

Facing the ballplayer, three feet away, was a two-inch profile of a dark-haired woman.

The crude mural seemed to suggest a visual parable about the relationship of Hall and Heady—he the all-powerful athlete, and she the small, insignificant object that mighty Casey had launched into space in his quest to hit a home run.

Colonel Hugh H. Waggoner, superintendent of the state highway patrol, had taken a portable radio into the death chamber as a security precaution. Radio contact was maintained with the prison yard, the deputy warden's office, and the contingent of patrol officers. As the execution moved toward its consummation, Waggoner advised his various posts of the progress. When he sent word that Hall and Heady were dead, several newsmen who had stationed themselves in patrol cars to hear the first reports dashed the fifty yards to the nearest phones to be the first to tell their editors that the notorious kidnappers were dead.

Warden Eidson later remarked that he thought everything went off smoothly. The executions were the eighth and ninth that he had conducted in the four and a half years he had held his position.

"It's a job I hate to do," he said, "but I wouldn't ask anyone else to do it for me."

Mrs. Tatman noted that she had planned to say something to Heady after she was strapped in, but "everything was going so smoothly I was afraid to for fear I would say something wrong."

She also said that she had not noticed any change in Heady's demeanour or attitude on the last day of her life.

"She told me that she knew I didn't like my job," Mrs. Tatman said, "but I had to do it. She thanked me. She also told me that she knew she had made a mistake and would have to pay for it."

Mrs. Tatman said that, considered as an individual and not as someone who had committed a murder, Heady seemed like a nice person. "She was very interesting to talk with and seemed to be an intelligent woman."

It was also revealed that both Hall and Heady had written letters of apology to the Greenlease family. The full text of Heady's letter to the boy's parents read:

Mr. and Mrs. Greenlease,
I doubt if this letter will do much good, but there isn't anything we could do or say that would atone for our mistake. I do hope it helps a little.

I would give anything if I could go back to that Sunday in September and erase everything that has happened since. It all seems like a nightmare to me.

We have always known that we would have to pay, but that doesn't return Bobby, but if it gives you satisfaction, then we won't be giving our lives in vain.

I don't say I don't enjoy money, as everyone does, but that was not my motive. I could have been very very happy with Carl living in my house as I had been, but he had been used to more money. My case was loving not wisely, but too well. I wanted so much for him to be happy.

I never realized that Bobby would be such a sweet child until it was too late.

I am not trying in any way to make any excuse for my actions. As I don't have any, but I think anyone will find if you drink from one to two fifths of whisky a day for a year and a half that your brain doesn't function properly. Since I have been in jail is the first time I've been able to reason clearly for some time.

I would like for the sisters to know I am sorry too, as their's is a wonderful faith.

I hope as time goes on it will help heal your hurt and that you find peace.

Yours resp.
Bonnie Heady

Heady was apparently referring in her letter to Sunday, September 27, when she and Hall supposedly finalized their plan to abduct Bobby Greenlease from school.

Hall's letter, written while the trial was in progress, was addressed to Robert Greenlease. He asked Dietrich to deliver it; but the lawyer felt that it was more prudent to wait until after the execution to make it public. "It was purely a letter is all it amounted to," Dietrich explained. In fact, though, Hall asked for forgiveness in the letter, and declared that he did not know where the missing ransom was. Robert Greenlease apparently believed him, and told reporters, "I no longer wonder if he buried it before his arrest." He also agreed with Father Evans that Hall seemed to express genuine contrition. "His statement has the ring of truth," Greenlease said.

Virginia and Robert Greenlease had not stayed up on the night of the execution to await word on the kidnappers' deaths, but had gone to bed early.

On the day after the double execution, indicted patrolman Elmer Dolan remained in custody in the Jackson County jail, where Heady and Hall had been incarcerated, in default of a $25,000 bond.

Heady was buried in a quiet, brief ceremony on December 19 in a cemetery in Clearmont, Missouri, north of Maryville, where she had graduated from high school. The ten-minute service was conducted in a graveside tent. Earlier that morning, Nellie Baker had gone to the Price Funeral Home in Maryville with a friend, Hester McQuate. Both women had been living in Heady's home in St. Joseph since the body of Bobby Greenlease was disinterred. The two women were briefly allowed to view Heady's remains. She had been dressed for burial in a beige-coloured suit with a brown flower design, and a brown scarf.

Others at the graveside service included Harold Hull and his wife, and Heady's uncle, Ed Clutter. Though she had many acquaintances in the area, and her ex-husband had been a successful livestock dealer who traded in Maryville, no one she had known in her former life showed up. Only a few spectators were on hand, and everyone was dry-eyed and silent. Baker, McQuate, and Clutter sent four sprays of flowers. The Reverend Franklin Kohl, pastor of the First Christian Church in Maryville, officiated. Heady had attended services at the church when she was a student at Maryville. After quoting some lines from the Bible, he read several lines from the poem *In Memoriam*, by Alfred, Lord Tennyson:

> *O, yet we trust that somehow good*
> *Will be the final goal of ill,*

To pangs of nature, sins of will,
Defects of doubt, and taints of blood;

That nothing walks with aimless feet;
That not one life shall be destroy'd,
Or cast as rubbish to the void,
When God hath made the pile complete; . . .

Behold, we know not anything;
I can but trust that good shall fall,
At last—far off—at last, to all
And every winter change to spring.

Heady's plain, bronze-coloured steel casket was then lowered into the ground. Her grave lay next to that of her father, beneath two pine trees on the top of a hill. Visible across the valley was the farmhouse where she was born.

Just minutes after midnight that same day, a hearse from the Torneden Funeral Home in Pleasanton, Kansas, arrived at the Buescher Funeral Home in Jefferson City. Around five o'clock that morning it departed for the return trip. When the hearse arrived in Hall's home town, Hall's body was transported to the hamlet of Turning Point, a short distance away. Marshall Hoag, city marshal John S. Fletcher, postmaster Lawrence Leisure, merchant Francis James, and retired telephone company executive Samuel Tucker served as pallbearers. The Reverend William O. Pfeiffer, pastor of the Pleasanton Presbyterian Church, officiated at the graveside service. Attending were Amos Hall, the eighty-three-year-old uncle of Carl Austin Hall, and two other relatives. Hall's body was interred beneath a one-ton granite tombstone on which was engraved simply the name "Hall." He was buried beside his father, mother, and brother. Nearby stood the granite obelisk commemorating the Marais des Cygnes Massacre that his grandfather Austin Hall had survived by pretending to be dead.

On December 29, the grand jury in Kansas City indicted Shoulders for perjury. Judge Richard Duncan, who received the indictment, set bond at $10,000.

10.

The Greenlease Curse

On the morning of New Year's Day 1954, former Cuckoo Gang member John "Buddy" Lugar was shot to death on a lonely road outside Madison, Illinois, across the Mississippi River from St. Louis. Just two hours earlier, at 6 A.M., he had gone to the Paddock, a notorious East St. Louis bar owned by Frank "Buster" Wortman. Wortman, one of the most powerful and ruthless underworld figures in the St. Louis area, lived in Collinsville, Illinois, in a house surrounded by a moat.

St. Louis police had recently questioned Lugar, an associate of Costello, about the missing Greenlease ransom money. He had spent New Year's Eve at a bar on St. Louis's DeBaliviere Strip, known for its nightclubs and bar girls. The police were investigating a report that the money was taken to a room maintained at the Roosevelt Hotel near downtown St. Louis by an associate of Lugar, who lived in the hotel. He had previously been part owner of the nearby Capitol Bar; June Marie George, Shoulders's landlady, had negotiated to buy it, but the sale fell through.

A week later, on January 8, Shoulders pleaded not guilty to

perjury charges in Kansas City, and posted bond. That same month, the FBI, in its ongoing search for the missing ransom money, announced that it was investigating Costello's finances. He was deeply in debt, the bureau had learned, and within the past three years borrowed more than $70,000, using his home and business as collateral. Mrs. May Traynor, a longtime operator of notorious brothels, loaned him $41,000 of that amount. Inexplicably, the police had found a notation of Traynor's address in the Arsenal Street apartment when Heady was arrested.

The unexplained circumstances behind Lugar's assassination, and the address notation found in Hall and Heady's rented apartment, are just two of many clues to a fathomless puzzle that, for more than a half-century, has defied solution: What happened to the $303,720 after Shoulders and Costello stole it, with the collusion of cabdriver John Hager and patrolman Elmer Dolan?

Did Hager contact Costello even earlier than on the afternoon of Tuesday, October 6? If Costello had then immediately contacted Shoulders, one or both of them might have gone to see Heady. Hager knew the address from the moment he met Hall. Hall had handed him an envelope addressed to Esther Grant at 4504 Arsenal Street, and asked him to arrange to have it delivered to Heady by another cabdriver. Did Costello hope to put his hands on enough cash to immediately repay the ex-madam? Was Hall's "hunch" that "Something's wrong" when he insisted on immediately leaving the Coral Court the correct one, after all? Unable or unwilling to suspect Hager, a fellow ex-con, of betrayal, had he nonetheless accurately sensed—even given the fact that he was paranoid—that something was amiss?

Moreover, what was the meaning of the mysterious exchange between Heady and Food and Drug agent Roy Pruitt, on the day before her execution, when she told him that she could explain how they obtained drugs, and added, "Carl can tell you all about the money, too." When Pruitt brought her into the corridor outside Hall's cell, he had reportedly said to her, "Shut up. We have already talked too much. Remember, we never rat on a pal." Back in her cell, Heady explained, "Carl and I have a pact. I cannot talk about the drugs or the money without his permission. And he has refused to give it to me. My lips are sealed."

Heady had made the same boast to others, including *St. Louis Globe-Democrat* reporter Ted Schafers. Yet the only "pal" in Hall's life before, during, or after the kidnapping was Hager. He had no other friend except for lawyer Bernard Patton, who was not a pal so much as a well-connected ally. But Hager had ratted on Hall, who would have regarded the cabdriver as a Judas after he contacted Costello. Or was the exchange between Hall and Heady merely an amusement they had improvised to bedevil the authorities, as many observers came to believe? If the testimony of two priests, seasoned defence lawyers Dietrich and Hull, Pleasanton lawyer Marshall Hoag, and assorted law enforcement and prison officials are to be credited, Hall and Heady were sincere in their repentance. Both seemed as genuinely puzzled as everyone else about what happened to the missing ransom. Heady's guess was that Shoulders stole the money.

Hall and Heady probably did not experience anything like profound remorse. That was almost certainly a moral quality neither was capable of attaining. There was a tinge of "if only" on both their parts—Heady wishing that she had been able to spend some of the ransom money on herself, if only Hall had not botched things up; Hall admitting as much himself.

Yet neither sought to appeal their sentence; both wrote letters of apology to the Greenlease family, knowing that they had nothing to gain; and they went to their deaths with a sense that each deserved their punishment. The suggestion that they took with them the secret of what happened to the ransom money leads down a labyrinth of conspiracy theories unsupported by the known evidence. The FBI, like the St. Louis and Kansas City police departments, rightly concluded that Costello, with the connivance of Shoulders, Dolan, and Hager, stole half the ransom money. The only remaining piece of the puzzle is how it was disposed of afterwards.

The lives of Shoulders, Costello, Hager, and Dolan spiralled catastrophically downward in the early months of 1954, as though the missing ransom carried with it a Pharaonic-like curse on anyone who touched it, or was involved in trying to hide or fence it. Dolan, testifying before a grand jury in Kansas City, said that he actually saw only one suitcase and a briefcase taken from Hall's apartment. He said he found out only later that the second suitcase apparently had been placed in the police car at an undetermined time. Shoulders now told the authorities that he asked cabdriver Hager to carry one of the suitcases. Hager dutifully remembered that indeed he had carried a suitcase to the police car. All three fabrications were brazen ex-post-facto attempts at a coordinated cover story that would contest Hall's version of events. If the missing ransom had been fenced to a figure far more powerful than Costello—possibly John Vitale, head of the St. Louis mob; or Buster Wortman—then all four had another reason to revise their story: They feared for their lives if the money trail led anywhere outside of the Newstead station.

On March 26, Shoulders, aged fifty-five, married his thirty-year-old landlady, June Marie George. It was his third marriage, and her second. The following month, he was sentenced to three years in prison for perjury. He later suffered a heart attack and was confined at the U.S. Medical Center in Springfield, Missouri. Two weeks earlier, Dolan had been sentenced to serve two years in prison, also for perjury.

In October 1954, ten months after Hall and Heady were executed, Costello was found shot and seriously wounded in his home. He told police he had accidentally shot himself in the left side of his chest while he was cleaning his gun—one commonly used for target practice—even though the time was 3:30 A.M., and no oil or cleaning implements were found nearby. Taken to Jewish Hospital, he subsequently told Chief of Detectives James Chapman that he had not shot himself, but refused to elaborate. He later retracted his allegation that someone had shot him, and insisted that he had wounded himself accidentally. Reporters and police officials close to the case believed that his wife, Barbara, had shot Costello during an argument.

Another incident that attracted the attention of authorities concerned some mysterious digging that occurred around Bland, Missouri, about ninety miles southwest of St. Louis, in January 1955. A man who gave his name as Allsmeyer approached a contractor's crew at a popular truck stop restaurant, Diamonds, forty miles west of St. Louis, and offered them $160 to "excavate a basement" on some property near Bland. But once they were at the site, the stranger directed the crew in what appeared to them to be rather aimless excavation. After several hours, he halted the operation, and was seen no more. It was later learned that the digging had been done without the knowledge or consent of the landowner, and the name Allsmeyer turned out to be fictitious. Crew members did not see the stranger remove anything from the excavation site. One theory was that he had returned later and removed something uncovered by the digging but not noticed by the crew.

On June 5, 1955, an Indianapolis lawyer named David Probstein went missing after leaving St. Louis. In a series of articles for *The Saturday Evening Post*, reporter John Bartlow Martin later wrote that the disappearance of Probstein and his possible tie to the missing ransom came to light during an investigation by ex-FBI agent Walt Sheridan.

"Sheridan," Martin wrote, "was working on the theory that Dave Probstein may have been a courier for the Greenlease money." A few of the ransom bills turned up in August 1955, about two months after Probstein disappeared, in towns between St. Louis and Chicago. Probstein had been associated with State Cab in

Indianapolis, which Teamster boss Jimmy Hoffa allegedly had an interest in. He was also associated with the Alder Insurance Company, as was Allen M. Dorfman. "Dorfman," said Martin, "is a Chicago insurance man deeply involved with Jimmy Hoffa and the son of a key figure in the Chicago underworld." State Cab was losing money, and two Teamsters from St. Louis—Ben Saltzman and Barney Baker—went to Indianapolis to look things over. "Barney Baker's former wife says that Baker told her he had to go to Indianapolis 'to take care of a shyster lawyer for Jimmy Hoffa and if he did this one more job for Jimmy, he would be close [to Hoffa] forever,'" Martin wrote. "Baker denies this." Baker was a close associate of both Costello and Vitale. The FBI believed that Costello fenced the money via John Vitale, according to Martin. Costello and Vitale had grown up together in the same St. Louis neighbourhood, and were friends.

Some police officials and reporters close to the case gave serious credence to the Vitale connection. In one scenario, Vitale bought the money from Costello and Shoulders for ten cents on the dollar, and sent it to the casinos in Havana for it to be put back into circulation. In another scenario, the money was distributed through carnivals in the Chicago area. That explained why some of the money turned up in that part of the country.

Also in 1955, Bobby Gene Carr, the son of Coral Court owner John Carr, was found dead in the trunk of his automobile in Illinois. The cause of death was multiple knife and gunshot wounds, which suggested that he might have been tortured beforehand. The younger Carr was a Korean War veteran who had worked as a cabdriver and novelty salesman, and his murder only fuelled public speculation that his father was involved in the disappearance of half the ransom money. Many people thought that the money had been stashed on the motel's grounds, or even secreted within the walls, perhaps by Hall, Carr, or someone else.

In May 1956, a federal grand jury in Kansas City subpoenaed Mollie Baker, the divorced wife of former Teamster hooligan and ex-convict Barney Baker, who testified, "Baker told me Joe Costello got the Greenlease money." The grand jury also subpoenaed Hager, but he refused to testify on grounds that he might incriminate himself. He was now living in Los Angeles, and receiving payments of about $200 a week from Costello. Previously, he told the *St. Louis Globe-Democrat* that Costello loaned him money occasionally—most recently when he needed $300 to get furniture and personal belongings out of storage in Los Angeles. Hager had remained in California, except for occasional visits to St. Louis, since early 1954. Also refusing to testify on the same grounds were Dolan, who had been released from prison in December 1955; Costello's wife, Barbara; and John Francis Kinney, a bartender and associate of Costello.

The grand jury then began to investigate Costello's so-called loans to Hager, and the mysterious digging in Bland. Costello refused to testify because he was under indictment on a charge of interstate transportation of firearms. Missouri police had found three revolvers in his glove compartment. Talking to reporters, he denied making regular payments to Hager since the cabdriver moved to Los Angeles, saying that he only once gave Hager $500 as a personal reward for his help in the arrest of the kidnappers, and after Hager's union had voted to give him a $500 reward.

According to Sue Ann Wood, a reporter for the *St. Louis Globe-Democrat*, and Judge Arthur Litz, a St. Louis magistrate, the *Post-Dispatch* sent court reporter John J. Hines to Los Angeles to find Hager, some years after he had moved to Los Angeles, and to offer him $25,000 in exchange for revealing all he knew about what happened to the second half of the ransom. A destitute Hager was living in a rooming house when Hines found him. After listening to the newspaper's offer, Hager walked to a window and for several long minutes simply stared out at the street, debating with himself. Finally, he turned to Hines and said, "I've told everything I know." Costello was a far more fearsome adversary than poverty.

Curiously, Costello provided financial assistance not only to Hager, but also to Dolan and Shoulders. Ace Cab mechanics also repaired June George Shoulders's car as necessary, always saw that it was topped up with fuel, and often furnished her with a driver when she went to visit her husband at the U.S. Medical Center in Springfield. She was also a frequent dinner guest of the Costellos. "For all his kindnesses," wrote reporter Thomas Yarbrough in the *St. Louis Post-Dispatch*, "Costello is getting to be known among investigators as 'Godfather.'" (Mario Puzo's bestseller *The Godfather* would not be published until 1969.)

"I help a lot of folks," Costello explained, regarding his financial assistance of Hager, though he denied making regular payments. "I'm generous," he said, "but not a complete idiot."

Costello's income, Yarbrough noted, was "not enough to enable him to throw money around recklessly, and in times past he has borrowed heavily."

Shoulders, who had told the grand jury in Kansas City that he would never again live in St. Louis, returned there when he left prison in an ambulance as a heart patient. According to published reports, he had taken an intense interest in religion while in prison, the Bible was said to be his favourite reading material, and he had even considered entering the ministry. Dolan was now working for a local building materials firm and as an attendant at a service station.

In July 1956 the *St. Louis Post-Dispatch* reported that, despite many promising leads, local and federal investigations into the missing ransom money had all come to a dead end. But the FBI had not given up. At one time, it had assigned sixty-five men to the case. "If the investigators sometimes wonder whether the thing is hopeless," wrote Yarbrough, "they can take heart in remembering that the Brink's robbery case—another one in which the bureau never called quits—took six years to solve."

Only 115 of the 16,971 marked bills, or $1,690 of the missing $303,720, had by now turned up, even though the serial numbers of the missing bills were nationally circulated by the FBI three weeks after the kidnappers were caught. The first bill showed up on August 20, 1954, when an airport employee in Minot, North Dakota, checked his money against a master list to while away the solitary hours of the night and discovered that the bill matched. Most of the other bills turned up in the Chicago area. All of the recovered money was returned to the Greenlease family. Investigators now believed that virtually all of the missing $303,720 had been put into circulation.

In May 1957, Shoulders and Dolan set up a dry-cleaning shop, but the venture, D. & S. Cleaner, failed and was sold a year later.

The following month, a grand jury in St. Louis subpoenaed Dolan's wife, Mary. She refused to answer questions on grounds that she might incriminate herself. One of the questions put to her by U.S. Attorney Forrest Boecker was: "Isn't it a fact that sometime during the past two years you have received loans or advances from Joe Costello in the form of $100 bills?" Another was: "Isn't it a fact that while temporarily deprived of your husband's support that you secured employment and also received loans from friends in order to keep your household going?" Further questioning by Boecker implied that Mrs. Dolan had bought a 1955 Plymouth through a Costello fleet discount, and that earlier she had driven a car registered to Ace Cab.

In August 1958, Sandra O'Day appeared for an hour before the grand jury. She had been in jail in nearby Edwardsville, Illinois, on a warrant charging her with assault to murder Garland McGarvey, and was brought to the federal building in St. Louis under a writ of habeas corpus. O'Day had shot McGarvey, a former convict and admitted former brothel owner, in his home in nearby Madison, Illinois, on April 4. Four years earlier, Buddy Lugar had been assassinated while driving near Madison on New Year's Day. In recent months, O'Day had been working as a prostitute out of

McGarvey's house. She had also been seen entering and leaving the Broadview Hotel in East St. Louis where Wortman maintained a suite. O'Day, who claimed she shot McGarvey to prevent him from further abusing Mrs. Garvey, was acquitted in June.

According to the *Post-Dispatch*, O'Day "answered questions readily, repeating answers she gave to questions at a previous grand jury appearance."

That same month, during hearings by the Senate Select Committee on Improper Activities in the Labor and Management Field in Washington, D.C., committee counsel Robert F. Kennedy interrogated Indiana Teamster official and ex-convict Gus Zapas. Kennedy did not mention the Greenlease kidnapping in his questioning of Zapas, but he had said weeks earlier that the missing ransom money would come up during the investigation of the gangster element in unions. Specifically, according to one line of thought, mobster John Vitale had used carnivals in the Chicago area as a means to put the ransom money back into circulation, as previously noted. The Teamsters were trying to organize carnival workers at that same time.

Noting that Zapas had been arrested in Chicago on October 23, 1953, in the company of two St. Louis hoodlums, Kennedy asked Zapas: "Did you ever discuss with anyone getting rid of some hot money you had for a few cents on the dollar?" Zapas replied: "No, sir." Kennedy: "You never discussed stolen or kidnap money?" Zapas again replied: "No." Among the spectators sitting in the rear was Teamsters president Jimmy Hoffa. Zapas also denied that he had threatened to kill David Probstein, the Indianapolis lawyer who had vanished in June 1955, but he did admit he had once thrown him out of his office because he was a "pesty little fellow" that "you wanted out of the way."

Costello also testified before the Senate subcommittee. He refused to answer Kennedy's question about whether there was a large statue of the Virgin Mary in his home, and that hidden behind it was a .38 calibre pistol.

Former "rooming house" operator May Traynor testified that Shoulders was never on her payroll, but said that she had given him payments of about $25 at intervals of every three or four months, and that other madams had done so as well. Ironically, Shoulders, as of August 1958, was the manager of four genuine rooming houses. Early that month, he was arrested in a case involving an alleged abortion on a twenty-five-year-old woman, but charges were dismissed.

In January 1959, just days before he was scheduled to begin serving a thirty-month sentence in federal prison, Costello attempted to take his own life with a drug overdose. Costello and his codefendant, Joseph J. Cannella, an Ace Cab supervisor, had been found guilty by a jury in the U.S. District Court in St. Louis of transporting three revolvers from Illinois to Missouri in violation of the federal firearms act that prohibited a person convicted of a felony from shipping firearms interstate. Costello had served a state prison term for burglary in 1936. Costello's wife, Barbara, worried about his growing despondency, was credited with saving his life. Realizing what he had done, she forced him to swallow coffee until he reached the hospital, where his stomach was pumped. Doctors later explained that Costello had taken one and a half times a lethal dose of a barbiturate, but the drug was contained in slow-dissolving capsules.

Another reason for Costello's depression was a $35,000 suit filed against him and his wife the previous September by Traynor, who was also a distant relative of Barbara Costello. The retired brothel operator claimed that she was fraudulently persuaded to release a deed of trust she held on Costello's home as security for a loan to Costello.

Father Charles Dismas Clark, SJ, known locally and later in a film of that title starring Don Murray as "the hoodlum priest," told reporters that he had visited Costello at his home the Monday before he tried to commit suicide, and found Costello sick with a severe cold. On Tuesday, he heard that Costello had been taken to the hospital, and tried to visit him, but was not permitted in the room.

After a three-day stay, Costello was released, and his physician reported that his patient's condition had not been as serious as first reported.

In the fall of 1961, May Traynor was found shot and beaten in her home. Costello still owed her $31,700, and they had had a falling out. "I just know Joe had something to do with it," she told police, who found her mortally injured. But before she died, she changed her story, and Costello was freed after questioning.

A popular theory among some political and police insiders in St. Louis about what happened to the ransom money was that Costello had immediately turned it over to Traynor to launder it. Costello had consistently refused to say where he had been on the night of Tuesday, October 6. If he had gone to Traynor's brothel and given the money to her for safekeeping, and ultimately arranged with her to launder it, that would explain why he had not been seen at his usual haunts. Traynor was known to have close ties with both Vitale and Buster Wortman in East St. Louis. Costello had borrowed money from her, securing the debt with mortgages on his cab business and his home. When detectives arrested Heady at the rented apartment at 4504 Arsenal, they discovered a slip of paper with Traynor's address. The fact that Traynor was beaten suggested that someone was trying to get information from her that she was unwilling to give.

One possible explanation to the Traynor puzzle is that Hager had not only alerted Shoulders and Costello that Hall was the probable kidnapper, but also that his accomplice was staying in an apartment on Arsenal Street. Shoulders, who claimed that he had been on a stakeout on the day of Hall's arrest, may have been telling at least a version of the truth—he may have been staking out Hall and Heady's apartment. When Heady abruptly left the apartment at 5 P.M. to buy whisky, milk, and cigarettes, Shoulders—and possibly Costello—may have entered the apartment to look for more ransom money. If money was found, Shoulders may have been directed to take it directly to Traynor for laundering—thus the piece of paper with Traynor's address on it that police later discovered in the apartment.

If Traynor had laundered the money, as Costello asked her to do, she may have short-changed him, and he subsequently found out about it. That theory would explain her retraction that Costello was behind the attack, because otherwise Traynor would be implicated in laundering the money.

The following February, Costello was arrested in the fatal shooting of Edward G. Brown, a thirty-year-old hoodlum, outside Brown's Tic Toc Club on St. Louis's DeBaliviere Strip. Brown had been found dying in the gutter in front of his club, with his head on the curb. Before he died, he told a patrolman that he and Costello had quarrelled over a demand by the latter that his cab company be given exclusive loading privileges at the club. An hour later, an intoxicated Costello—his trousers, overcoat, and shirt collar splattered with blood—showed up at the emergency room of Barnes Hospital with a bullet wound in his left forearm. An unidentified young woman had driven him. He said Brown had shot him in a quarrel, but he did not know who shot Brown—claiming he did not even know the other man had been shot. At an inquest, a policeman testified he had heard Costello admit the shooting. Costello was subsequently indicted for second-degree murder.

Shoulders died in May 1962 of a heart attack at Jewish Hospital in St. Louis. After his release from prison, he had suffered from bouts of depression and bitterness.

Costello, described by the *St. Louis Globe-Democrat* as "the unwilling star of the Greenlease ransom melodrama," died at his home of a heart attack at age fifty-three in July 1962. He had been under treatment for hypertension, diabetes, liver trouble, ulcers, and sinus headaches, and for a time was under psychiatric care. Although associates claimed he was bankrupt and owed money to everyone, his home was tastefully furnished and a Cadillac was parked outside. He had spent twenty-three months in federal prison on the federal firearms charge, and was due to stand trial on the second-degree murder charges on September 5.

Despite the promise of a presidential pardon, ex-patrolman Elmer Dolan refused to reveal everything he knew about the case until after both Costello and Shoulders died. In September 1962, the FBI flew Dolan to Washington, where he confessed that Shoulders had given half of the ransom to Costello before the two policemen took Hall to the Newstead Avenue police station. He confirmed that Costello had been the mysterious third man that Hall had seen in the corridor on the night of his arrest at the Town House, but added a new twist—there had also been a fourth man. This unidentified fourth man—not Hager—was possibly the person in Hall's hotel room that Shoulders briefly spoke to while Dolan was escorting Hall down the corridor. After Hall was booked, Dolan further confirmed, both policemen separately drove to Costello's home, where Shoulders offered him $50,000. This same mysterious fourth man also attended the basement meeting. Most likely he was an associate of Costello, or perhaps of Traynor, whose function was simply to provide extra security while the money was being moved from location to location.

Dolan had lied, as almost everyone involved in the case suspected, because he feared for his and his family's lives. Although he did not accept hush money from Costello, he did take $1,500 from the mobster after he was released from prison because he had been granted his freedom at Christmastime, and had a wife and six children to support. President Lyndon B. Johnson, at J. Edgar Hoover's urging, pardoned Dolan in 1965. Dolan died in 1973.

The missing money was to remain a black mark against the corruption-riddled St. Louis Police Department for years. The FBI met with a similar lack of success in its attempt to find out what happened to the stolen half of the ransom. Director Hoover assigned agent Howard Kennedy to work full-time on recovering the money. He spent fifteen fruitless years on the assignment.

In August 1972, Shoulders's son, Louis D. Shoulders, was murdered while he was staying at a resort in the Missouri Ozarks. Car bombings were a favoured method of execution of the St. Louis underworld, and the younger Shoulders died when he turned on the ignition of his Cadillac. Police speculated that he had been killed in retaliation for the murder of Edward Steska, the business manager of Pipefitters Local 562, a corrupt union at the centre of a protracted power struggle. Wortman controlled the union, and Shoulders had been a bodyguard on the local's payroll. Shoulders's pallbearers included James Giamanco, the reputed new head of the St. Louis Mafia. From 1962 through 1981, the St. Louis area was rocked by nineteen car bombings, or about one a year, leaving thirteen people dead, leading the *St. Louis Post-Dispatch* to call St. Louis "the unofficial car bombing capital of the country." Most were hoodlum-related.

(In a sad postscript to the Shoulders saga, the *Post-Dispatch* reported in June 2007 that the body of a homeless woman named Susan Jansen had been found at a local recycling centre. She apparently fell asleep in a Dumpster, and her body was later crushed by a recycling truck's compactor. Susan was subsequently identified as the daughter of Louis D. Shoulders. She and her husband, Thomas Jansen, both heroin addicts, were often in trouble with the law, and had recently been evicted from their home. Some time later, Jansen's missing husband turned up dead on a conveyor belt at a recycled paper factory in Arizona. Both apparently had been crushed in the same recycling bin.)

Arthur Reeder, a member of the FBI's special kidnapping squad who led the interrogation of Hall and Heady, took their statements in which they admitted their guilt, and read Hall's confession at the trial, committed suicide at his Denver home in August 1981.

John Carr passed away in 1984, bequeathing the Coral Court to his widow, Jesse, and their longtime housekeeper, Martha Shott. Route 66, bypassed in 1975 by U.S. Interstate 44, was now a back road, and the motel itself had become a seedy outpost used mostly by adolescents for one-night stands. Although listed on the National Register of Historic Places, the motel fell into disrepair and was demolished in 1995 after it was sold to a developer to make room for a generic subdivision. The Museum of Transportation in St. Louis did manage, however, to preserve a complete two-room bungalow.

The Greenlease case led most schools to enforce a new policy whereby parents had to sign cards providing the names of individuals who were permitted to remove a child from school in the event of an emergency. A rash of custodial wars in the 1970s between feuding parents also led to a series of unlawful kidnappings, with the result that schools were faced with an even more complicated problem of who was authorized to remove a child from school. Despite new technologies for preventing or foiling a kidnapping—for example, inserting a microchip in a child's book bag—nearly a million children in America are currently listed as missing.

Robert and Virginia Greenlease, Bobby's parents, found consolation and refuge in their Catholic faith. They frequently visited the Abbey Mausoleum in Forest Hills Cemetery, and were often comforted by Father Joseph Freeman, a Jesuit who taught philosophy and theology at Rockhurst College. They later funded a professorship in the priest's honour, provided funds for a library and an art gallery, and in 1962 donated land for the construction of a high school on the college campus. Robert Greenlease passed away at his home in Mission Hills on September 17, 1969, just a few days before the sixteenth anniversary of Bobby's abduction, at the age of eighty-seven. When Virginia Greenlease died at age ninety-one, in 2001, she left $1 million each to both the college and the high school in the names of her husband and Bobby. Though both parents lived into old age, Bobby's adopted older brother, Paul, and his sister, Virginia Sue, who as an adult struggled with drug addiction, never quite recovered from the tragedy; both died in their forties.

In early 2002, the Greenlease estate was auctioned off. Dutch, English, and French oil paintings, French fainting couches, crystal glassware, hand-painted china, and a seven-carat diamond ring were among the highlights. During the estate sale, in the Grand Ballroom of the Fairmont Hotel in Country Club Plaza, waiters in tuxedos and crisp white aprons served guests. Five hundred people attended. All proceeds went to Rockhurst University, which Bobby probably would have attended had he lived.

The French Institute of Notre Dame de Sion in Kansas City's Hyde Park is now known as the Notre Dame de Sion School, and is managed by a lay board. Unable to attract a sufficient number of new members in the United States, the congregation of Notre Dame de Sion no longer supplies the school with teachers. Its relationship with the school is in name only. Soeur Morand, the nun who delivered Bobby to Bonnie Brown Heady on Monday morning, September 28, 1953, never recovered from the kidnapping and was haunted by guilt all her life. Unable to be dissuaded that she was not responsible for Bobby's fate, she frequently burst into tears at the mention of his name. Like all of the other nuns at the school, she eventually returned to the congregation's motherhouse in Paris.

Sources and Acknowledgments

In October 1953, I was a high school freshman in St. Louis, and lived a half-block away from the Newstead Avenue police station where Lieutenant Shoulders and Patrolman Dolan brought Carl Austin Hall and Bonnie Brown Heady after they were arrested. I vividly recall the crowd of reporters and onlookers gathered outside as the two kidnappers were being processed and interviewed within. By curious coincidence, as an even younger boy I had lived only a few doors away from the house on Arsenal Street, across from Tower Grove Park, where Hall and Heady holed up after arriving in St. Louis from Kansas City, and where Hall abandoned a drunken Heady in search of the good life and a hooker. A Jesuit uncle of mine taught at Rockhurst High School.

A few days after Hall and Heady were arrested, and news of the missing ransom became the talk of the nation, my father drove my two brothers and me to the grounds of Kenrick Seminary, not far from the Coral Court motel on the old Highway 66, where he had once studied. Hundreds if not thousands of people were now scouring possible sites where Hall might have hidden the missing money. My father's theory was that few people even knew about Kenrick's heavily wooded grounds, which were not open to the public, and that Hall could not have found a more hidden and yet convenient place to bury the money. For several hours, we tramped the creek beds and woods, searching for signs of recently upturned earth before Dad reluctantly decided that most likely the money was hidden elsewhere.

Over the next few years, the subject of the kidnapping and the missing ransom money continued to turn up occasionally in daily conversations and in news reports. My father managed a bookstore, where I clerked during college, and among the customers were reporters and detectives who had covered or worked on the case. Most notable of these was John J. Hines, a reporter for the *St. Louis Post-Dispatch*, who had written a number of front-page stories on the kidnapping. From time to time, some of us would gather in the back room, where Dad always kept a bottle of wine for his favourite customers, and the conversation would sometimes drift to the Greenlease case. Hines liked to tell about the time he interviewed Shoulders, who menacingly spun the barrel of a loaded revolver during the course of the interview in an effort to intimidate him. Hines, who stood a hulking six foot six, was merely amused. Since Hall and Heady had both been executed, the only matter of speculation in the aftermath concerned who had taken the missing half of the ransom money. The consensus then as now was that, acting on orders from Joe Costello, Shoulders had stolen it; Dolan had been a patsy who refused to point an accusing finger at the police lieutenant because he feared for his own life and that of his family; and Costello quickly laundered the money, with everyone having a different theory about how exactly he went about doing that.

I later moved from St. Louis, but the Greenlease case remained a persistent and even haunting memory. It was not any desire to solve the mystery of the missing ransom that ultimately impelled me to write this book. That would be a fine feather in any reporter's cap, yet it is a relatively minor detail in an unspeakable tragedy. It is also a chapter that can never be written because the handful of people involved in the disappearance of the money are long dead, and have taken their secrets with them.

My goal in writing this book was to provide the first definitive account of the Greenlease case, one of the worst crimes this nation has ever seen, and thereby to restore to public memory the last terrible day of Bobby Greenlease's life; to chronicle the sorrow of the Greenlease family and their friends; and to document the crime, punishment, and first steps at rehabilitation of a psychopathic murderer whose only motive, like that of Raskolnikov, was greed. I have written it without feeling the need to embellish. The stark chronology of this uniquely American tragedy speaks all too sombrely for itself.

Two extraordinary examples of in-depth reporting of a major event in our national life during the 1950s were the exhaustive coverage of the Greenlease case by the reporting staffs of *The Kansas City Star* and the *St. Louis Post-Dispatch*. This book could not have been written without those two indispensable resources. Other primary sources included the extensive confessions obtained from both Carl Austin Hall and Bonnie Brown Heady, and the thousands of pages of related investigative material, contained in the FBI's *Greenlease Kidnapping Summary Report*; court transcripts of the *United States v. Hall and Heady* murder trial; statements given by Carl Austin Hall and Bonnie Brown Heady on November 30, 1953, in the Missouri State Penitentiary to St. Louis chief of police Jeremiah J. O'Connell, circuit attorney Edward L. Dowd, and FBI agent Dan Walters; St. Louis Board of Police Inquiry, "Interim Report: Lt. Louis Shoulders—Ptn. Elmer Dolan," February 2, 1954; and *Elmer Dolan, Appellant, v. United States of America, Appellee,* U.S. Court of Appeals, Eighth Circuit, January 21, 1955.

Other print and Internet resources were the archives of the *Chicago Tribune, Detroit News, Detroit Times, Jefferson City News-Tribune, Kansas City Daily Record, Kansas City Times, Life, New York Times, New York Herald Tribune, Newsweek, Pleasanton Observer-Enterprise, St. Joseph News-Press, St. Louis Globe-Democrat, St. Louis Star-Times,* and *Time.* These sources were also consulted: James Deakin, *A Grave for Bobby: The Greenlease Slaying,* New York: William Morrow, 1990; East St. Louis Action Research Project archives; David Krajicek, "The Greenlease Kidnapping," *Crimelibrary.com*; William O. Luton, Jr., "The History of Route 66 and the Coral Court," *Isuzoperformance.com*; J. J. Maloney, "The Greenlease Kidnapping," *Crimemagazine.com*; John Bartlow

Martin, "The Struggle to Get Hoffa," *Saturday Evening Post*, a seven-part series running from June 27 to August 8, 1959; Patterson Smith, "Ransom Kidnapping in America," *AB Bookman's Weekly*, April 23, 1990; and Anselm Theising, Ph.D., "The Beginning of Organized Crime in St. Louis," *Riverweb.uluc.edu*.

In instances where there were different or conflicting accounts of an incident, a date or time of day, or a conversation, I have used my best judgment to decide which version to use.

During my research, I visited Pleasanton, Kansas, and St. Joseph, Kansas City, Boonville, and St. Louis, Missouri. Along the way, I took notes and scoured archives. I am grateful to the research staffs of the Kansas City Public Library, the St. Louis Public Library, the Missouri Historical Society in St. Louis, the archives of the Mercantile Library at the University of Missouri St. Louis, and the New York Public Library for their generous assistance.

I am also indebted to Charles Brown, Martin Duggan, Dolores Friesen, the Honorable Thomas Grady, Colonel Jim Hackett, Matt Heidenry, Donna Korando, the Honorable Arthur Litz, John McGuire, Mickey McTague, Ted Schafers, and Sue Ann Wood. I had a very special conversation with Judy Haudrich, who was a student at the French Institute of Notre Dame de Sion on the day Bobby Greenlease was kidnapped, and who shared her memories, insights, and a brief memoir of that traumatic time with me. My wife, Pat, helped me with the archival research in Kansas City, St. Louis, and New York, and gave the manuscript the kind of exhaustive, constructive editorial scrutiny that challenged every lazy sentence, unproven assertion, or complicated story line. I could not have written this book without her patient, loving support. My other first readers were, as always, my four children—Mary, John, James, and Margaret—whose close readings also provided me with invaluable advice and editorial judgment. I am also grateful to my editor, Michael Flamini; assistant editor Vicki Lame; and copy editor Fred Chase for their indispensable help; and to my agent, Andrew Blauner, who found this fifty-year obsession of mine a very good home. To all of you, my very deepest thanks.